Arnhem and the Aftermath

Dedicated to any future generation in a World of the Free, of whom my grandchildren Daniël, Robijn and Iris Kuiper are dearest.

Arnhem and the Aftermath

Civilian Experiences in the Netherlands 1940–45

Harry Kuiper

Pen & Sword
MILITARY

First published in Great Britain in 2019 by
Pen & Sword Military
An imprint of
Pen & Sword Books Ltd
Yorkshire - Philadelphia

Copyright © Harry Kuiper, 2019

ISBN 978 1 47387 098 7

The right of Harry Kuiper to be identified as Author of this work has
been asserted by him in accordance with the Copyright, Designs and
Patents Act 1988.

A CIP catalogue record for this book is available from the British
Library.

Typeset in Ehrhardt by
Mac Style
Printed and bound in England
By TJ International Ltd.

Pen & Sword Books Ltd incorporates the Imprints of Pen & Sword
Books Archaeology, Atlas, Aviation, Battleground, Discovery, Family
History, History, Maritime, Military, Naval, Politics, Railways, Select,
Transport, True Crime, Fiction, Frontline Books, Leo Cooper,
Praetorian Press, Seaforth Publishing, Wharncliffe and White Owl.

For a complete list of Pen & Sword titles please contact

PEN & SWORD BOOKS LIMITED
47 Church Street, Barnsley, South Yorkshire, S70 2AS, England
E-mail: enquiries@pen-and-sword.co.uk
Website: www.pen-and-sword.co.uk

or

PEN AND SWORD BOOKS
1950 Lawrence Rd, Havertown, PA 19083, USA
E-mail: uspen-and-sword@casematepublishers.com

Contents

Acknowledgements

My nieces, nephews and other people deserve my thanks for having shared their war-time memories on behalf of the manuscript of this book. Most were living in Arnhem and the area between 1940 and late September 1944, and were evicted like my parents and myself. While most of us were born in the thirties, we were young when events caught us by surprise and made a great impression on us. For many young children, real war-time experiences can be mental baggage for the rest of their lives. This has resulted in very strong personal memories with each of those interviewed. Next, a few dairies could be used. These and some other original documents are in the hands of their children, who all became more invaluable sources of this truthful book.

They were experiences on the smallest possible scales. We all, however, knew reasonably well about each other's war-time experiences. They were often relived in family circles. Fortunately, all those interviewed were available for a number of interview sessions. The advantage was that common personal experiences were explained which, when twisted or mixed up with other memories, could be evaluated by others without much reserve. Here, they are placed against the back-ground of the greater events of this war.

Chapter One

Pig Food in Those Days:
Seasoning the Aftermath

Tasteless thin porridge, cooked in rye and too much water, became a standard lunch-time meal at our home in January 1945. This was during the Hunger Winter in the western part of the Netherlands. My parents had found accommodation with my grandmother in the small town of Breukelen, north of Utrecht city. The population of Arnhem, our home town, and a number of neighbouring towns had been evicted, following the German repulse of British and Polish forces involved in Operation Market Garden in late September 1944.

Once the Allied soldiers were out, Arnhem and a few nearby towns were treated as spoils of war by the Germans. About 170,000 civilians involved were evicted within one to three days. The city and a number of neighbouring towns such as Oosterbeek were deserted; virtually no citizens were left. Germans, mainly from the Ruhr, were encouraged by the German occupiers and some Dutch collaborators to take anything they wanted from private houses, shops or any kind of store. Furniture, bedding and other common household property were taken 'to compensate for what German families have lost in the Allied bomb raids' as they reasoned. They left with trucks and trailers loaded, as secretly taken pictures show. The city's stockpiles were removed as well, as much as possible. Wehrmacht and SS officers took wines from shops and animals from Arnhem's zoo for sumptuous party dinners. Certain kind of ladies were paid with jewellery and fur coats stolen from shops, as hidden eye-witnesses recorded.

At the same time, common provisions were no longer available north of the country's main river, as the Germans purposely blocked all food and coal supplies to the western part of the country. The Nazi purpose was to starve as many as possible. About 4.5 million people suffered from this man-made famine, which also had nothing to do with Market Garden. Moreover,

1944/45 was a very cold winter; 20,000 to 25,000 citizens are believed to have died and by early May 1945 many were on the verge of starving. Others, especially youngsters, have been affected by hunger all their lives. The actress Audrey Hepburn, who lived in Arnhem during the war as a young teenager, was one of these. This author and most compatriots interviewed for this book experienced the same kinds of fate.

Porridge cooked in rye and water was a mucky replacement of any minimal meals as offered in the soup kitchens of most towns. The grey and somewhat brown porridge without a grain of salt or sugar – because, who had salt or sugar? – was just disgusting. Citizens of Amsterdam joked about the situation in their own way. 'If I had bacon', they would say to each other, 'I would prepare bacon and eggs, if I had eggs.' Next to the taste of the porridge, there were the sharp husks that filled my mouth with every reluctant little bite. When finished, a crown of husks covered most of the rim on my dish. But a crown of distaste, that is what it really was. For most months during the Hunger Winter in early 1945, it was one of only two or three daily meals. A dish of porridge in rye and water was too little to survive on and too much to die from, even for this 5-year old. For many decades it was one of several bad memories of the Second World War.

One day and very angry with this filthy porridge as usual, I exploded. '*Ik vreet die rotzooi niet meer*' (I shall eat this nasty scrap no longer). Silence followed. Because what was that from this little boy? Nasty scrap? And: '*vreet*' (as larger animals like pigs do) instead of 'eet', as decently brought up children are supposed to say? That was unheard of! That might deserve a stern reprimand; like from a Dutch uncle, as the British say. There was no uncle and no reprimand. For a moment, my parents looked at each other and hesitated. Just by nodding, my father left it to my mother. She could not disagree with me and said in a soft voice, 'You better eat it, dear son! People in Amsterdam don't have anything to eat at all.' And this was true. Pictures show youngsters in Amsterdam scraping dustbins in the streets during this Hunger Winter.

For decades after the war, I could recall the nasty smell and taste of porridge of rye and water, just by thinking of it, as others in this country could recall the smell and the filthy taste of fatty tulip bulbs they ate in their particular case, to survive the worst part of the German occupation. In 2009,

I mentioned this war-time experience to a farmer who lived in the East of the Netherlands, just in passing, as an anecdote. They had suffered far less from food scarcity and he stared at me. 'Porridge of rye and water?', he said in a compassionate voice. 'In this area that was pig food, in those days.'

Pig food. At his words, a feeling of undeserved shame fell over my shoulders.

Chapter Two

1938 – Peace without Effort

Being a seagoing trade nation for centuries, but at the same time a small country with a correspondingly small population, the Netherlands has maintained a policy of strict neutrality in international matters since 1815. Neutrality had become a questionable policy during the years prior to 1940, both towards the Dutch population and to Germany. Neutrality meant not only that the Dutch Army was an unpopular weapon but that the country's defences were in a rather poor state.

For strategic reasons, Germany had considered occupation of the Netherlands in the First World War. Germany's natural disadvantage in the northwest with regards to its defence north of the Rhine was a reason to consider violation of the Dutch neutrality. Germany's Imperial High Command supported the idea strongly. The Germans did not fear the Dutch themselves, but German records show that they were concerned about a potential British invasion on the Dutch coast and what side the Dutch would take in such an event. Such an invasion would have led to the destruction of dunes or dikes which would have resulted in the flooding of up to 60 per cent of the country by the sea. One third of the Netherlands is below sea level, minus 6.76m (22ft) at the lowest. Since the Dutch have been fighting the sea for centuries, causing 'wet feet' as they call it is not how to make friends there, but it definitely would not help the Germans either.

The Germans felt safer when the entire Dutch coast and the many open waterways in the southwest were in their hands. It would have created another German front at the same time, or a larger western front at least. Emperor Wilhelm II rejected these proposals, perhaps out of sympathy with his fellow ruler, Queen Wilhelmina. The Germans would not have accepted it. But the Dutch government would not have allowed it either.

The core area of the Dutch defence in 1939–40 was called Fortress Holland, although of course the country is actually called the Netherlands.

This defence mostly faced the east and the south, not the west. The fortress refers to the western part of the Netherlands, covering most of the two provinces of Holland, from Dordrecht as far north as the naval base Den Helder, and included cities like Rotterdam, The Hague and Amsterdam. Fortress Holland's easternmost limit was the Grebbeberg Line in the centre of the country, which included Utrecht city and a large part of Utrecht province. One army corps was quartered inside Fortress Holland. This included the defence of cities and the coast line. Two more corps (four infantry divisions each) were at the German border which is about 250 km (150 miles) long. One corps was quartered along the Belgian border. Just as in the First World War, any violations of Dutch air space, territory or national waters were resisted.

Hitler gave two reasons for wanting the Netherlands. One was that he preferred the German Reich to be a fully self-supporting nation in every respect, an *autarky* as he called it. He wanted to avoid the risks of any food and oil supply shortages in case of a future war, as he had said before, even as early as in *Mein Kampf,* his political and racial outline of 1924. These shortages, unforeseen before 1914, had emerged as huge problems in Germany and Austria during the First World War and for many years after. As a second reason, Hitler wanted to secure the Dutch, Belgian and some French sea ports in view of an invasion of Great Britain.

What Hitler did not mention is that Germany, heavily dependent on strategic commodities from Swedish ore and Ukrainian grain to Dutch oil and vegetables, could be an *autarky* only if such imports could be purchased at prices far below market values, to further benefit the German economy. Militarily, Hitler and his generals believed that the Netherlands was an easy prey. This was because both the country and its population were small and most people led by senior politicians were averse to militarism. Hitler also wanted Luxemburg and Poland, as he announced in this same conference. There was continuing political trouble between Germany and Poland, in fact since 1919.

The Netherlands meanwhile was on the verge of reaping the fruits of their own variant of Neville Chamberlain's words after his return from his meeting with 'the German Chancellor Herr Hitler' in Munich, on 30 September 1938. 'Peace for our time', were his words that evening. The

Dutch equivalent seemed to be
'Peace without effort'.

In the deep economic crisis of the
1930s, Dutch trade relations with
Germany were not obstructed by
reports of large-scale rearmaments.
No senior Dutch army officers
spoke out about the situation from
their point of view, to mobilise
public opinion in the interest of
improving military defence. It was a common theme in the 1930s for the
governments of various countries not to stand up to Germany's bullying,
nor to prepare for war. The miserable Dutch policy of neutrality during
the thirties while serious threats and rumours of war increased, backfired
as much as those of neighbouring countries and resulted in the damage to
much life and property in each.

Peace without effort. Dutch symbol from the
twenties and thirties showing a broken rifle.

Until the outbreak of war, rivers and artificial floodplains were considered
useful handicaps to keep hostile land forces out. In 1794–5 however, the
French just waited for frozen rivers. On the eve of war, there still were
the age-old Dutch Water Lines, which were potential flood land areas but
by that time, aerial warfare meant that nowhere was safe any more. These
potential flood land areas were to be found between the southernmost points
of the IJsselmeer and the Meuse, as extra lines of defence in the middle of
the country, facing the east. A parallel water line was to be found just east
of Utrecht city. In the south, the Dutch and similar Belgian defences were
not connected.

Most of the Dutch territory east of these water lines, including the IJssel
River from the Rhine to the IJsselmeer, was considered hard to defend. This
compares with the German challenge to defend a similar and bordering
countryside. In the Dutch case, a substantial part of the population in the
east and north and their properties, about 40 per cent of the country, were to
be abandoned just like that, even though the citizens had paid for a reliable
defence.

The Grebbe Line was a long strip of land to be flooded as a defence,
alongside a narrow stream called Grebbe, about 30 km (20 miles) west

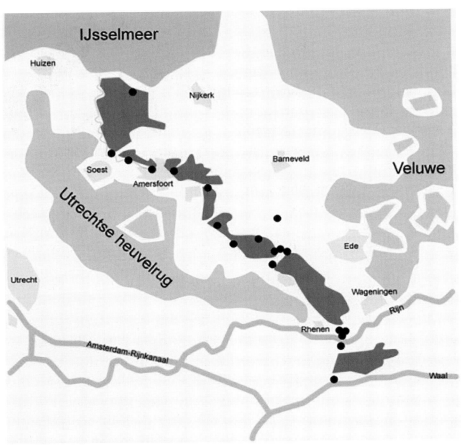

Dutch defences between the IJsselmeer, Rhine and Waal rivers, 1940. Grebbeberg is between the towns of Wageningen and Rhenen.

of Arnhem. Both the defence line and the narrow stream are situated transversely to the Rhine, between the small towns of Wageningen and Rhenen. At the same time, it is about the shortest road and rail distance between the German border and the North Sea at Scheveningen, at just 155 km (93 miles). Next to the Rhine there is a natural elevation of 52m (171ft), called Grebbeberg. Lacking any real mountains, the Dutch tend to call every elevation a 'berg' or mountain. Locals particularly use these terms, though many just call their steep local elevations 'bumps', including those up to twice as high as the Grebbeberg or 'Mount Grebbe'.

Even before Hitler's statement of May 1939 that he wanted the Netherlands, the Wehrmacht had acted on his 'wants list'. Officers had already started to monitor the Netherlands, Belgium and Luxemburg. German officers in plain clothes simply took trains and travelled to Mount Grebbe, to air bases and to major bridges as well as The Hague, Rotterdam, Moerdyk and other points of military interest. They observed, noted, took pictures and even managed to map mine-fields. They found out about areas to be flooded and realised that planes and paratroopers could easily bypass these areas simply by flying over them.

After May 1945, detailed maps were found showing the remarkable amount of intelligence the Germans had collected. One showed areas fit for flooding. One showed all major telephone and telegraph lines throughout the country on which it was hand-written that this particular map might be very useful for the Wehrmacht.

Several members of the cabinet, as well as in some political factions, were incredibly naïve and could not believe spying or even aggression from the Germans, when reported from several sides. Reports and protests in the Dutch Parliament were not effective. A look-out tower on top of the Grebbeberg, as part of the playground in the zoo, was used by the 'visitors' to take more pictures and make notes of the Grebbeberg defences below them. It was not closed as members of parliament demanded. Dutch Prime Minister Dirk de Geer, who was anything but a courageous political character, reasoned that it might 'hamper the commercial interests of the playground owners'. The tower, now removed, was still there

Booted Dutch Military Police on guard in a country rich in water, November 1939. Were they expecting German soldiers to arrive on wooden rafts?

after the war, as I remember from a very early class trip. It offered a very attractive, very wide view in all directions.

Two German air force divisions were organized and trained according to Reichsmarschal Goering's guidelines of creating a force of parachutists and airborne troops. When Goering was informed about Hitler's resolve to attack and conquer the Netherlands, in January 1939, he proposed deployment of his airborne forces. His new and prestigious force enabled Germany's military planners to develop an all-new strategy by combining land and air forces.

The Germans selected four targets in the Netherlands to be attacked from the air and bypass the many waterways. If successful, they were to be relieved by ground forces. These targets were two sets of bridges, at Dordrecht, southeast of Rotterdam, and the very long Moerdyk bridges south of this city; the Nieuwe Maas River bridges of Rotterdam and the city itself. Targets in The Hague were capturing Queen Wilhelmina, the Dutch cabinet and the Armed Forces High Command.

Chapter Three

1940 – *Fall Gelb* – Case Yellow

The Dutch view of the world was dramatically changed from 4am local time on 10 May 1940. A total force of 750,000 made up of Wehrmacht and Waffen-SS regiments prepared to break the Dutch border north to south. Additionally, 1,150 Luftwaffe aircraft were to steal the show in the west. The German operation to invade the West was code-named *Fall Gelb* or Case Yellow. A deployment like this was a first in military warfare. The invasion of the Netherlands was the responsibility of the German 18th Army, formed on 4 November 1939. Basically, this new army was intended to defend Germany's western border between the Rhine and the North Sea coast.

Hitler had ordered the invasion on 9 October. He had reiterated his friendship to the Netherlands and Belgium only three days earlier. In a meeting on 17 January 1940 Hitler reaffirmed his actual plans to his generals. Army Group B was the second of three, all assigned to *Fall Gelb*. Its major assignment was to take a small part of the Netherlands only (the Maastricht area) then attack Belgium and advance to the French coast near Calais. Since the devastating Thirty Years War (1618–1648) in what became Germany only in the nineteenth century, young men from these areas had migrated to the Netherlands each summer, to earn themselves a living their homelands were unable to offer. Since Hitler came to power, these young men were turned into merciless enemies.

Army Group B invaded the Netherlands at six different places. The German thrust in the two central attacks aimed westward, parallel to the Rhine, Waal and Meuse rivers. North of the Rhine, two infantry divisions were launched. About half of this force was supposed to advance towards Arnhem crossing the IJssel River, a branch of the Rhine. The second thrust of attack was south of the Meuse, a few kilometres south of Nijmegen. The city was taken without any Dutch resistance.

A second German assault south of the rivers involved two infantry divisions, plus a reserve. Its tanks were to relieve the airborne forces at the Moerdyk bridges south of Dordrecht, before moving on to Rotterdam and The Hague.

The campaign of the Netherlands was believed by the Germans to be comparable to the lightning strike against Denmark. In the German perception, the Dutch Army was not a real challenge either; they calculated that they would need one or two days before the Dutch were ready to surrender. They could then move their troops to Belgium and Northern France to face the French and the British Expeditionary Forces. Germany's 6th Army advanced to Maastricht in the south. Once the bridge on the Meuse at Maastricht was in their hands, they could enter northern Belgium. Not far to the south, German airborne troops took the Belgian fortress Eben Emael easily.

The first real defence line against ground attacks from the east in the central part of the country in 1940 was the so-called IJssel Line. The first move from the Germans was to send waves of medium bombers, transport aircraft conveying soldiers and small armament, and fighter planes as a protective force. In 1940, the Luftwaffe was one of the most dangerous weapons in the German arsenal. They flew over the country but once over the North Sea and seemingly out of sight, most planes turned back for the real objective, an attack on the Netherlands from an unexpected west. It caused the first encounters of the day, as some Dutch fighter planes had been ordered to take to the air.

Marius, my father, did his job under a peculiar-looking standard-issue helmet. As a volunteer in the Dutch Air Guard Service, it was his duty to scan the skies and to report German planes. Until the Dutch Army's surrender on 15 May, this service reported over 16,000 foreign planes in the Dutch skies. His station was at a heavy two-piece blockhouse, called Fortress IJsseloord which was between the road and rail bridges across the IJssel River near Arnhem. It guarded the three bridges that stood closely side by side, of which two were for trains, with a single track each. It was the most important railway link with Germany.

In particular he had to be careful of planes attacking the bridge. He did not have any help in carrying out his duty from futuristic-sounding equipment like radar screens, even though the Netherlands was one of the countries where radar was being developed secretly, since 1934. He just had to keep both eyes and ears wide open, under the blue skies of what very many have remembered as a beautiful morning, just before Whitsun, the holiday which comes six weeks after Easter. Could Marius, 29 years old in early May 1940, be expected to be capable of stopping part of this whole avalanche of German power once the Nazi juggernaut started? It was not his job to blow a bridge, so the answer is: No.

In these early hours of the morning in this very quiet and rural part of the country, Marius was one of the thousands who could hear an unusual heavy buzzing rumble far from Arnhem and unfamiliar, terrifying sounds of impact. It was not quite four o'clock; dark and, apart from the distant sounds, totally still. If anything remarkable, significant or otherwise nefarious had to be reported by Marius, there was an army telephone in the blockhouse. Little had been reported so far. My father lacked any standard military training and he was unarmed, but well-instructed. His two elder brothers had served many years earlier and Marius was out legally. But he believed this was unfair towards his brothers and when it looked like Germany was growing to be a military threat, he wanted to be available for the Dutch defence. Not rejected for being too young in 1936, he was admitted as a volunteer at the age of 27.

Professionally, Marius was a baker. He was employed with his own father, Harm, who was 64 years of age in 1940. Both age and the deep economic recession of the thirties had caused my father to join the business and retrain, to master the art of baking. As a master baker himself, Harm still worked every day at the bakery which was situated in the heart of Arnhem, just below the sturdy tower of the Eusebius church. This tower is Arnhem's proud, late-gothic landmark, dating back to 1450. The tower was 85m (259ft) tall in 1940 – and until 1944! Marius was supposed to take over and continue his father's bakery and the modest staff for production and sales, at some undefined point in the future; they had planned that it would happen around 1945, maybe. I was not greatly attracted by his job. My other grandfather was a publisher and I loved to listen to him when he told about his former business trips to book fairs in Leipzig and Frankfurt.

Marius was supposed to present himself in uniform at his station when circumstances called for, if not summoned beforehand. Such circumstances were either a special order, or his own judgement of a developing situation calling for action. As a baker, he was used to getting up in the middle of the night, every night except on Sundays. It made him a useful soldier, as many military attacks start early in the morning. Political tensions were high in the late thirties; rumours of war came in every day. It became clear to the Dutch from all over the country that 'matters were serious'. One day in early May, Marius told his father: 'Dad, I have to go'. His father understood. Later that day after having put on his uniform, Marius left his wife Alida and their 8-month-old son. He pedalled to the IJssel bridge, to man his station.

Alida was far from happy, of course, about all that could happen to Marius under the threat of an imminent war. She would not be able to see him and bring him little extras, as the area of the bridge was totally restricted. 'Goodbye, Mas,' she said, which was short for Marius. 'Goodbye, and may God be with you.' Like everyone else, she remembered the awful stories of the Great War from a quarter of a century ago, that her parents and older brothers had told her. After this had come the Spanish Civil War; now it seemed to be her turn in life to face an ordeal. What was she to expect?

It was only a few days later that the German war machine embarked on the ground and spat mercilessly from the air. At Arnhem, the German border is little over 20 km (12 miles) away. Somewhere between the IJssel bridges and the German border, a group of twenty-one soldiers were the first to show up in early daylight, on bicycles. They were dressed in familiar-looking uniforms. Strangely enough, they had not been noticed or reported by Dutch military at the border. War is not just the butcher's art of killing the enemy and inciting the enemy to violence. It is the Janus art of misleading as well. Who were these silently pedalling guys?

They were halted by an even smaller but very suspicious group of Dutch soldiers, who had not been notified of such a military group in the area. Immediately, the Dutch soldiers presented arms to them. Were they Germans who had been hiding somewhere in the Netherlands for a while? Had they taken a sneaky route to cross the border early on that same day? There was more to it than rumour, as Hitler himself had ordered to have uniforms stolen from surrounding countries. But how to steal many foreign helmets, clearly seemed to be more of a challenge and they were as often as not what gave the game away.

The strange-looking armed men showed their passes. Their commander said that they had been ordered to cycle to Apeldoorn, a town 26 km (15 miles) north of Arnhem; or, to put it in a different perspective, Apeldoorn was a mere 30 km (18 miles) to the north of the IJssel bridges, even though the officer did not say the word 'bridge' at all. But what was to be found in rural Apeldoorn? Could they really be trusted, having come from the German side? Only the commander spoke Dutch and it was noted as well that none of the other men said a word. It is true that their bicycles gave them a rather Dutch appearance. But then, on closer inspection, they looked like being dressed in bad imitations of Dutch military police uniforms. Finally, their dark blue Dutch helmets appeared to be made from cardboard. Because of their fake helmets it suddenly became abundantly clear that these soldiers were no Dutch soldiers. So they could have been shot instantly.

Instead, they were arrested, so quickly that there was no time to resist. They handed over their weapons, rather than attempting to use them. German weapons! They must have been acting under orders. When interrogated on the spot, it appeared that they were soldiers from the SS *Standarte Der Führer*, a tank division. Their orders were not to go to Apeldoorn, but to eliminate the Dutch force which was protecting the IJssel bridges near Arnhem. Their mission had failed and they were taken prisoner. But only twenty minutes later, another 100 to 200 *Standarte* members showed up. They were heavily armed and on roaring black motor cycles with sidecars. They freed their imprisoned comrades and in turn arrested the Dutch.

Chapter Four

Capturing Arnhem

The IJssel branch of the Rhine near Arnhem forms a natural barrier between Arnhem and Germany. Arnhem borders both rivers on the north side. The city is surrounded by a commuter belt of rather well-heeled small towns. Arnhem was – and still is – a provincial capital with a head-count of almost 100,000 in 1940. Of the roads out of Arnhem, two lead to Germany. Five different Dutch Army units were stationed in Arnhem just north of the city. There were civil and military courts, prisons and a number of hospitals, including one military. In spite of its strategic significance, Arnhem is considered to be hard to defend because of the surrounding high ground.

At the time of the invasion, not a single Dutch field gun or other piece of armament was in place to fire at the Germans at the IJssel bridges early in the morning of 10 May. The absence of artillery shelling was undoubtedly due to the shortage of long-range artillery and ammunition.

To reach Arnhem from Germany, the German Army had to capture the rail bridges and the parallel road bridge on the IJssel, and wipe out the Dutch defensive positions. Artillery at the IJssel bridges consisted of four field guns dating from 1894, six machine guns and charges to blow up the three side by side bridges. The number of regular soldiers and those few to observe the skies amounted to about thirty men. Some were detailed to blow up the bridges. Demolition charges were in place. So, if the Wehrmacht did show up, the blockhouse and its Dutch complement would receive them very warmly. Tension was high, had been very high, in fact, even since the first days of April. Rumours that the Germans might attack spread daily.

Such rumours were soon proved to be correct. One colonel in Germany's Counter-Intelligence, the Abwehr in Berlin, a man who thoroughly despised Hitler and his Nazism, conveyed all data relating to the Netherlands and Belgium and when they were to be attacked to a Dutch military attaché in Berlin. It was high-treason, of course, but to the often sceptical Dutch, it should have been a godsend. Colonel Hans Oster's information also mentioned that the Germans planned an attack by paratroopers and airborne forces around The Hague and other places. That information was rejected out of hand at Dutch General HQ in The Hague. Some officers in the High Command said that they would welcome Germans from the air on pitchforks; it was an example of poor intelligence or extreme naiveté at least, which of course time has shown was very ill-advised.

According to Oster's information, Queen Wilhelmina was to be arrested and taken to Berlin. But, at the same time, Hitler postponed the date of German attacks of the Low Countries about twenty times. The result was that Oster's information, which was in fact very reliable, was not accepted in The Hague. In particular, no-one believed that the Queen, as the Dutch head of state, was to be arrested. One of the very few who *did* believe it was Queen Wilhelmina herself!

Belief in rumour was fed by the discovery of Germany's final plans for 10 May, *Fall Gelb*. They were found in the suitcase of a German officer whose aircraft had been forced by bad weather into an emergency landing in Belgium on an inland German flight to Cologne on 10 January. Copies of these plans were sent from Brussels to The Hague on the same day, but they were ignored by one of the highest commanders in the Dutch Army.

Three side-by-side rail and road bridges on the IJssel River, near Arnhem, as they looked from 1904 to 1940. The Germans entered from the left; the blockhouses were on the far right. The length, about 550m (1,675ft), is similar to many of those across the major rivers of the Netherlands. The pasture to the left is called a winter bed, and is designed to accommodate the overflowing waters in the dark, winter months.

Minutes after my father had returned to the blockhouse from his observation duty, the officer ordered the road and rail bridges to be blown up. Thundering explosions could be heard miles off. The noise reached up over the hilly slopes of Arnhem and neighbouring Velp, waking everyone who might still be asleep. The mayor of the seven communities of which Velp, just east of Arnhem is one, ordered an instant evacuation of half the population (those living closest to the IJssel bridge area) during the next few days. The IJssel bridges near Arnhem were not the only victims of violence; all the bridges across the IJssel, all the way to the IJssel Lake were blown up, explosion after explosion, with no exceptions. The Germans, however, had come prepared with many small boats for a quick blitz towards Arnhem.

Not very long after the explosions, the German trains arrived as expected and pulled up at the damaged bridge. The train appeared to be an armour-plated steam engine which pulled a mix of non-armoured passenger and freight cars. Later in the war, they often pushed one or a few flat cars to protect the engine from mines, while the first car or cars behind the engine were open, gondola types carrying anti-aircraft guns and men. At the IJssel, this train stopped close to the blown-up bridge and could only be used to fire. Several hundred metres behind the armoured train, the unprotected freight train stopped as well. It stopped partly on a viaduct, within the small town of Westervoort. This train carried manpower and supplies. The viaduct spanned the narrow main road from Germany to the IJssel bridge and Arnhem.

The armoured train was subjected to heavy fire from Fortress IJsseloord as soon as it was spotted. This continued for several hours and was also directed towards individuals and groups of four trying to cross the river in their small boats. After some time, the Dutch weapons became overheated and stuck. To cool them down, the soldiers reportedly emptied their bladders on them. It worked well and the firing continued. At Westervoort, across the IJssel, a Dutch detachment was in place near the railway embankment. They had been ordered not to fire until ordered and so they had waited; they now received telephoned orders from Fortress IJsseloord to open fire on the armoured train that had stopped before the IJssel bridge. The train thus was to come under siege from two banks.

By mistake, the Dutch at Westervoort opened their heavy machine gun fire on the second train, the freight train with manpower and supplies on the viaduct, standing almost right in front of them. According to accounts from people living nearby, the results were horrific. Ammunition supplies exploded and many Germans were killed both by the Dutch guns or by their own explosives. Many more were severely wounded. Ear piercing screams from the freight train could be heard all around, bringing the locals out, despite the noise of the firing and the bullets flying.

Once the firing had stopped, local people observed blood dripping from the floors of the freight train, and from the bullet holes in the sides of the wooden wagons, according to Dutch military reports, written shortly after, as well as a railroad report. Without having fired one shot themselves, these early German invaders had been given a fierce reception. The viaduct was a bridge too hot, their freight cars had become slaughter-houses. It took several hours before the battered freight train could be withdrawn, along with the useless armoured train. Both were taken back to Germany. In most other cases except for one, the deployment of armoured trains in the Netherlands proved a blunder. Had the bridge not been blown up, the armoured train would have thundered through Arnhem and continued another 40 km (25 miles) westward, in order to take up position near an overhead railway crossing and take part in the attack of the Dutch Grebbeberg positions.

Next to the fortifications on the banks of the IJssel were several small concrete walls, firing points across the river. From Fortress IJsseloord and from the banks, the Dutch fired on the Wehrmacht units which tried to cross the IJssel in their small boats. The Wehrmacht, of course, fired back at the blockhouses, but several boats were shot and sunk, taking the four occupants with them in most cases. Some men managed to stay afloat, swimming quickly with the tide. Fort IJsseloord must have been packed with bullets because the Dutch firing continued for several hours. But then, from an unexpected direction, men of *SS Standarte Der Führer*, arrived. They had crossed the IJssel a number of kilometres downstream, up north, in similar small boats, to take the bridges near Arnhem from the other side as well.

Several Dutch among the small garrison inside and around the blockhouses were hit. The SS then invaded the blockhouse and shouted: *'Waffen nieder!, Haende hoch!'* ("Weapons down! Hands up!") and the firing stopped. At least ten Dutch soldiers inside had been killed. Fifteen able-bodied stepped forward. A few more were severely wounded but happily my father was unharmed. The survivors were taken as prisoners of war and all were made to stand against a wall with rifles pointed at them. They were all grubby and much hard of hearing thanks to the noise of the guns, but the Dutch had put up such a spirited resistance that it was now 9.30am – nearly five hours after the first shots were fired had elapsed before they surrendered.

The Wehrmacht suffered many casualties from the Dutch guns, both at the viaduct and the IJssel bridge. As usual however, their exact number is not known, as the Germans never revealed casualty numbers. As Dr. Christian Zentner, German historian and journalist, states in his comprehensive book *Der Zweite Weltkrieg* (The Second World War, 1996): 'In reports of the Supreme Command of the Wehrmacht, numbers of Germans killed in action never emerged.' It isn't any different from the First World War, but it is exceptional in the case of a people otherwise known for meticulously keeping all other kinds of records. Most known killed in action figures are estimates by the Allies.

Having survived the ordeal was one thing, but what might lie ahead was another. The prisoners taken at the IJssel bridge were all worried. One Dutch soldier, who understood German, overheard two SS men discussing what to do with this small group of POWs, after their resistance and after having blown up the bridges in front of the Wehrmacht as well. Shoot them on the spot? Why not? Would anyone be able to tell the difference between men being shot within the walls of the blockhouse or on the premises outside (which is what the Germans did a week or so later, when British POWs were shot in barn near Bethune, in north west France)? Would anyone care at all? They had probably not yet been told of what had happened at the viaduct on the other side of the IJssel, or they would not have hesitated even for a minute.

After the prisoners had been lined up for several hours, the SS men decided, perhaps out of character, to act in line with the Geneva Convention and take their prisoners away to barracks in Arnhem. These POWs were lucky, or a few children would have known their fathers from pictures only. The SS in particular, even though they looked rather civilised in their pre-war black uniforms, became involved in all kinds of serious crimes, including the murders of unarmed civilians. As they were not regular soldiers, these professional killers, the dregs of German society, ignored international conventions. The Nuremberg Trials in 1946 declared the SS as an illegal and criminal organisation, citing the fact that 'The shooting of unarmed prisoners of war was general practice in some Waffen-SS divisions.'

Most reliable reports about this invasion were those of the city tram drivers who operated six routes within the city. Employees were able to report rather early in the morning whether or not they could finish their sections according to schedule. In most cases they could, although at first the overhead power supply was broken for a while all over the city. One exception was an interruption of the tram line from Oosterbeek through Arnhem to Velp. An explosion destroyed an overhead railway viaduct, just west of Arnhem. The viaduct crossed the road to and from Oosterbeek. The tram route was broken until the remnants of the viaduct had been removed and the overhead wires repaired, a few days later.

The explosion was a small one, but close to the long railway bridge which connects Arnhem and Nijmegen across the Rhine. It consisted of two double track truss arches and six double track deck truss bridges, having a total length of 466m (1,528ft) between abutments. One arch of this bridge was blown up by the Dutch Army even though the bridge was not under attack. At about the same time, both rail and road bridges at Nijmegen on the Waal were also blown up. The road bridge there was only four years old. When completed, the arch was the biggest single steel span in Europe. Nijmegen's current arch is the original one, as it was lifted and repaired during the war.

The easy conquest of Arnhem was an agreeable surprise to the Germans. The first units entered Arnhem about 11am. Spectators lined the streets when SS forces and their trucks arrived and took up positions with the Wehrmacht. They had constructed a temporary bridge across the IJssel at the city of Zutphen, some 30 km (20 miles) to the northeast. In Arnhem, the locals were terrified at seeing Hitler's much feared Wehrmacht on their own streets. Many spoke in whispers, as my parents told me much later. Now and then, however, a few sympathizers showed up and cheered. A new era had arrived, they screamed. No doubt about that. But a better one as a result of foreign military occupation?

In Arnhem, Germans faced only some minor skirmishes at the Rhine bridge in the city, the one to gain fame over four years later. But Dutch forces blew up the original bridge of 1935 at about 10am, as a precaution, even though no German forces were reported coming from Nijmegen, in the south. This bridge was identical to the one of September 1944. Arnhem's population took pride in this costly bridge, a high crossing to allow Rhine barges which are taller usually than other inland navigation ships. It replaced a narrow, centuries old pontoon-bridge some 200 metres downstream. Now the city's pride was a mess of warped steel beams in the water, blocking all Rhine traffic at the same time. The steel and wooden, somewhat swaying, pontoon-bridge had been kept in place however, as a reserve. It was reinstated quickly. The Germans ordered a repair of the road traffic bridge. It was completed in August 1944, less than a month before Market Garden.

During the next few hours the city became crowded with marching and loudly singing German units. They blocked public transport, even certain streets and squares entirely. By noon, the first German units, notably *SS Standarte Der Führer*, had reached Arnhem's west side speeding to Oosterbeek and beyond, towards the defensive Grebbeberg. All this was the outcome of the fighting around Arnhem in 1940.

Three major bridges and one viaduct in the Arnhem area were destroyed by the Dutch Army, while only one of these had been attacked. There was no serious Dutch defence of the city and consequently very little damage was done. There were not a great many casualties among the Dutch soldiers. In Nijmegen another two big bridges were destroyed by the Dutch, without an enemy in sight.

Comparable damage had been inflicted on other railway bridges all over the country, often as a precaution, without being threatened by German forces. In a board meeting of the Netherlands Railways on 8 June 1940, it was reported that a total of eighty-two rail bridges had been destroyed, including twenty-six long bridges of which fifteen were on major waterways. This referred to railway bridges only, as a number of major roads and bridges in the National Motorway Plan were still under construction or on the planning boards. Of course, far more damage was inflicted on Netherlands Railways property, engines, various kinds of rolling stock and buildings.

This included a lot of mindless destruction as well, such as steam engines driven into turntable pits.

The small number of POWs from the IJssel bridges was not properly taken care of. All prisoners, many of whom were scarcely trained under simulated warfare conditions, were in shock because of the long hours of fighting. My father was one of these. All were very thirsty, because of the heavy gun smoke. All were hungry and bathed in perspiration. There was no Red Cross to call on even if they had been allowed to help. German medics took care of the wounded Dutch and Germans themselves.

Early in the morning, the residents of Arnhem had first heard rumours and then the sounds of fierce fighting at the IJssel Bridge. Hours later, reports of men wounded and killed started coming in. But there were also those who had been captured. Where would they be? Were they in German hands and on their way to Germany? Were they even alive? Relatives from far and wide wanted to find out as soon as they could. Alida, my mother, was one of those. It was only during the afternoon that the captured Dutch were ordered to march to one of the barracks in Arnhem. At one point my mother, extremely anxious, was notified that POWs had been transferred from the IJssel bridge to army barracks not far from where my parents lived, with me in a cradle. Marius was believed to be among the POWs. Quickly, she collected together a few personal items for him, then rushed to those barracks.

At the gates surrounding the barracks, she asked any prisoners she could find if Marius was among the many Dutch POWs. And was he still alive? But all she got was, 'Marius who? Never heard of him'. This was not surprising as Marius had not spent much time at Fortress IJsseloord in the last few months. Only a few knew him. Initially, he was actually reported as missing, in official records. Suddenly however, Alida saw her Marius in the distance – standing at the wire fence, looking nonplussed at the outside world that was his own city. What an enormous relief and comfort for Alida! They were happy to see each other and kissed through the gaps in the wire fence. They could praise the Lord, they were relieved for now. But what was next?

Marius was kept a prisoner and sent to Germany in a convoy a few days later. Did my mother see him when the convoy left? I do not remember my parents having told me, but I am sure they did. He was transported by ordinary freight train, as was the German habit during the war for large groups of imprisoned people over long distances, such as POWs and Jews. As will become clear, there were no seats or benches, let alone toilets, in ordinary freight cars and many had to travel while sitting on the wooden floor, standing or leaning erect in the crowded cars. Food or drink were not provided, regardless of travelling time. Marius was interned at Sachsenhausen, 'The Camp for the Capital', 40 km (25 miles) north of Berlin.

Sachsenhausen was special. It had been opened in 1933 when the Nazis came to power, as a camp for German politicians, trades union leaders, journalists and dissidents. From this moment, Hitler's Nazi Party was no longer a political party in Germany, but an organisation determined to establish dictatorship and control all sections of society. The same fate would befall foreign countries when they were invaded. All other political parties and politicians were removed from public life, and subjected to continual humiliation during their imprisonment. Why was Marius in such company? The choice of Sachsenhausen was strange, since he had never been active in politics, the trades unions or the media. But he suffered the same privations as the other inmates. Later, dissidents were not the only ones held captive at Sachsenhausen. It is possible that he was sent there because of verbal or even physical resistance to German soldiers, since he was not a man to give in easily. Certainly, this was suggested to me many years later by other former POWs, as the reason for his being sent there.

Today Sachsenhausen is a museum showing examples of Nazi horrors. It appears to have been a truly hellish place in those years. All camps were staffed by the Totenkopf SS. Some particular Nazi instruments of torture and killing within the grounds have remained in place. One is an instrument in a pit, where prisoners were tied up in a standing line by their feet. Ropes around their necks were attached to round beams hanging half a metre above them. The beams could be wheeled round lengthways, one man wheeling at each end. So when the beams were wheeled, the skulls of the victims were simply ripped off their spines without the bodies being torn apart. The bodies were then thrown to one side, until they were carried off by other inmates, to be buried anonymously in large pits. When it rained, the SS-members just took shelter amongst their fresh victims.

This cruel appliance was used particularly for the killing of imprisoned Russian officers, though they did not arrive until late June 1941, so my father probably did not see this machinery. What he did see and experienced daily, was the way POWs like himself were treated, the appalling food and the terrible conditions they lived in, summer and winter. It was something of which he preferred not to speak; he refused, like so many others who have suffered from traumatic experiences in Nazi hands. The only things he has mentioned a few times is that the packages my mother sent him, via the International Red Cross, containing items like soap, towels and some clothing, were never delivered to him.

Fortunately, he was not in Sachsenhausen for long, as was the case with so very many. It has not been possible to trace exactly how long he was there, since the archives at Sachsenhausen were burned by neo-Nazis in 1992. He was transported to Stalag IIA at Neubrandenburg. This was a true POW-camp, just 100 km (62 miles) north of Sachsenhausen and is no longer in existence. My father's papers show that he was released from here on 11 January 1941. Most other Dutch POWs taken to Germany had been released on 5 June 1940. He was given a train ticket and went home, as it seems in the company of other released Dutch POWs, under the patronage of the International or Netherlands Red Cross. This was a journey of some 700 km (435 miles), so it may have taken more than one day, and probably overnight before he arrived in Arnhem. The only money he had in his pockets when released was 29.25 guilders, just three pounds sterling at that time. He spent it on food.

His return to Arnhem was a total surprise, as he had not been able to notify anyone. Suddenly, someone in the street called my mother, 'Now look, Marius is here again!' And was he the only one to be released? Perhaps, although compared to most other Dutch POWs, his captivity was a rather long one. Sachsenhausen was horrible. It continued to be used as a camp by the occupying Soviet forces until 1949. Once home, Marius looked emaciated and he coughed deep and continuously – all day, very loudly. He never lost this cough, not until he died at Christmastime, 1954. He had never done so before the war, an aunt told me later. His *joie de vivre*, his sense of humour, and his former desire for a large family had all left him, at least for the duration of the war. Many other families also chose not to have children in this period. Many got their next child only when the war was over.

One surprise when Marius returned, was that the Germans had taken over two prominent restaurants in Arnhem for the use of their own officers and men. One was prominently situated in front of the city's concert hall, called Musis Sacrum. A large sign at the front said it all: *Wehrmachtheim* or Army Home. The other one was called Café Royal. Here, Germans also met their Dutch friends of all kinds and levels.

On a summer's day, which may well have been a Sunday, in 1946, Marius took me to see what remained of Fortress IJsseloord. He showed me the structure and the ridiculous metal gate which was meant to scare off the Germans in 1940. It was still in place in 1946, next to the railway embankment. He told me all about it. The useless gate had survived a world war, doing as well as the neighbouring heavy steel door to block the railway. The gate was not the only barrier in 1940. On the other bank of the river a series of holes had been drilled in 1940, through the approach bridge's road surface. Steel beams, the height of a man, had filled the holes. These dragon's teeth, 'asparagus sticks' as the Dutch called them, might have stopped even the heaviest tanks, but not individual soldiers as long as the bridge was in place. These obstacles were removed when the bridge was repaired in November 1940.

The railway gate became a show piece in the war museum of Overloon, which was a battlefield in 1944, when the British 11 Armoured Division, known as the Black Bulls, engaged the Germans. In 1980, the blockhouse on the right side of the road bridge when leaving Arnhem became a monument, and was painted grey. Grenade and other damage all around have remained clearly visible. A concrete wall and a large white marble stone were erected, dedicated *To those who fell,* the standard phrase in the Netherlands after 1945. The stone lists the names of the fourteen men killed there on 10 May 1940.

Chapter Five

Confronting the Invader

The massive German strikes against the Netherlands all caused great confusion. Newspapers nervously issued 'extra bulletins'. Only the radio network could distribute the latest news quickly and country-wide, but military censorship had been effective since late August, 1939. It hampered the public in getting a fair picture of what was going on. It also hampered the work of newspaper and radio correspondents throughout the country from the start. But it also caused problems for the Germans and their collaborators.

The first major German success was to cause widespread fear and confusion among the population, when the Luftwaffe bombed a number of airfields, military defences and communication centres in the west. They created a flow of reports which alarmed the Dutch. In the same early hours, the Germans managed to capture a railroad bridge on the Meuse near the small town of Gennep, some 20km (12 miles) south of Nijmegen, without even inflicting any damage. It was just 8km (5 miles) from the German border. It was successful largely because of the use of stolen Dutch uniforms and fake helmets, which enabled them to continue their second overland advance and relieve airborne forces at the south of the Moerdyk bridges.

Between Arnhem and the Grebbeberg are Oosterbeek, Heelsum, Renkum and Wageningen. At Heelsum, two young people watched as the first German units of the 10th Army (Hamburg) and *SS Standarte Der Füehrer* entered their town. They were a 14-year-old girl Jo Richter and a 7-year-old boy, Gerrit Lourens. As several members of my family lived in or around Arnhem, all our war experiences have made great impact on us and were recalled and discussed many times after. It was a comforting experience to speak to all of my relations when preparing this book, because we were in a position to correct and remind one another of details if needed. Most memories are to do with our decreased living conditions at the time. They are of human interest, small images against the much greater picture of the war.

In one of those round-the-table interview-conferences, Jo recalled:

'We had heard the noises of the war since early that morning of 1940. It was in the afternoon when we could watch the first German troops as they entered our town, Heelsum. They were about a hundred. They rode motorcycles with side-cars, drove armoured vehicles and trucks. While they passed by, they fired their arms at windows now and then, as if they suspected opponents there. Or maybe they just wanted to overawe us anyway. No, we were not afraid and we did not hide. We had done nothing wrong, had we? But in a shop at a nearby corner suddenly all window panes shattered. The shop was a bakery! This happened at other houses as well.'

Gerrit was standing along the same road and watched the columns of grim-looking Germans and their vehicles, one after another, as they passed. Gerrit, younger and somewhat scared, held his grandfather's hand tightly. He recalled:

'The motorcades were impressive, but it turned somewhat different when these storm troops were halted for some reason. This was such a frightening sight to me, these men in their black uniforms, that I wrenched away from my grandad's hand and ran home.'

Grebbeberg is situated between the towns of Wageningen and Rhenen. In both towns the mayors, well aware of the risks to their citizens while close to a potential front line, executed an evacuation of the entire population with immediate effect, exactly as in Velp, but with the difference that at Wageningen and Rhenen the order of evacuation had come just a few days before 10 May. So, Piet Holleman, a 5-year-old boy from Wageningen, tells how his parents and many others reported at Wageningen's small harbour on the Rhine one morning very early to enter a special Rhine barge. The vessel sailed downstream to an agricultural polder-style municipality called Groot-Ammers, near Gouda. It was at Groot-Ammers where a very Christian population had prepared temporary shelter for families from Wageningen as long as they might need it.

The Holleman family found shelter with a famer's family. There were no relatives, friends, or otherwise there. They were people who reached out their hands to an unknown neighbour in the sense of the Bible. The Hollemans were not exceptionally lucky, as these reassuring experiences were shared by most other families from Wageningen as well. As war and German suppression progressed, readiness to help others increased throughout the country – although sadly not in all cases, nor in all places or under all conditions.

A few weeks later the Hollemans were allowed to return. Wageningen had suffered little from the sudden German advance. The town was at their rear when they attacked. Yet there was a difference. Since the Dutch Army needed field of fire to the east of the Grebbeberg defences, several houses and fruit-trees in front of the Dutch had been cut down. This damage is still visible in the older houses to this day.

German shelling of the Grebbeberg started in the evening of 10 May and also damaged the small town of Rhenen. This city, over 1100 years old, is situated 8km (five miles) west of the Grebbeberg. The shelling continued the next day along with hand to hand fighting at the Grebbeberg, while the town was bombed by Stukas, the Luftwaffe's tactical dive-bombers. Fortunately, the population had just been evacuated and the town was largely ruined, just to intimidate the Dutch forces behind the front lines. The Germans expected to break through the Grebbe line in a single day, regardless of their small majority and because of their very intensive espionage.

The battle for Grebbeberg took three days of hand to hand fighting. The German troops were up against the strong patriotic resistance of the Dutch, in spite of their poor equipment and poor leadership. Queen Wilhelmina said on 12 May that she would rather leave The Hague and 'stand in the trenches of the Grebbeberg to fight the Germans' than have the battle lost. The Germans finally broke through on 13 May. The Dutch withdrew to a third, much more westward line of defence and the next day, sadly, the atrocious bombing of Rotterdam definitely turned the tide for the Dutch. More than any other battle-ground in the country, the Grebbeberg has become a national symbol of the Dutch Army's resistance in 1940.

Two of the Dutch soldiers at the Grebbeberg were conscripts, Johan Kuiper, aged 35, from Zuidwolde and Cor Dubbes, aged 25 from Rotterdam. Conscripts were called into service wherever needed in the country, not necessarily in their own local area. Cor Dubbes, who later married into my family, became a successful manager of a factory making trams and railway stock in his battered home-town. He passed away in 1988, aged 73, but his memory will always live on.

Johan Kuiper had left the army in 1924 but was recalled in 1940 and he was put into an infantry regiment as a trained machine gunner at the Grebbeberg. Johan was my father's cousin. On 8 May, he sent a letter to his wife saying that he expected to be home again within a few days. He would have been most welcome, since she was in her last month of pregnancy after a still-born baby in 1938. It was a cheerful letter, disguising the fear he really felt. Johan did not come home again. He is still there. His regiment was in the thickest of the fighting and he was killed on 13 May. The circumstances are not known. He was one among 425 Dutch soldiers killed or missing.

The large number of victims within a couple of days in the same area was another shock to the country. In fact it was almost inconceivable to many Dutch in 1940 that 'such a thing could happen even in the Netherlands'. A few days later, both Dutch and German soldiers as well as many bereaved relatives from all over the country, combed the area to recover bodies and to look for those missing in action. Dutch soldiers, disarmed but still in their uniforms, were ordered by the Germans to bury the dead. The Germans were experienced in recovering soldiers killed in action. For the Dutch, this was the first such experience since Waterloo in 1815, unless they had served in the Netherlands East Indies. Some were familiar with the graveyards in Belgium and Northern France from the First World War. They did not know how to create a place like that themselves.

For weeks, Johan's wife and family anxiously tried to find out his whereabouts. Where and how was he; was he in Germany as a POW? In a hospital? Was he being taken care of by loyal citizens? Had he fled or escaped somewhere somehow? Not a single piece of information arrived. His brother and a family friend finally took to their bicycles on 31 May and pedalled some 150km (95 miles) to the Grebbeberg. There they searched and talked

Recovery of those killed in action at the Grebbeberg. The two men lying in front wearing puttees, their heads covered, are Dutch soldiers. Germans standing nearby wear caps and boots. The man with an armband, on the right, is a Dutchman. It is likely that the dark man in the middle is also Dutch. Grebbeberg, around 15 May 1940.

to others in the area. No one could confirm anything whatsoever. It was so very sad.

On 11 June Johan's son was born and he was named after his father. Only then did the searching relatives find a sergeant major in the area who had just been released himself. He sadly had to tell them that Johan Kuiper was killed in action. It was the very last thing that Johan's brother and his friend wanted to hear and they had to tell Johan's wife their sad news. His body was not found in the woods, or amongst those already buried, and he was not listed in any records. This was the fate of just one man amongst the millions killed in this war.

Continuous searching in the woods of the Grebbeberg area and at the site of the provisional cemetery resulted in some progress. Many family names in the Netherlands are spelled differently for which there are many reasons.

Kuiper is an age-old surname and there are several varieties. But a different spelling, like Cuypers, also means another genealogy. Many outsiders pay little attention to correct spelling and write the surnames as they believe are correct. When buried, Johan's surname had been a victim of such slovenliness. His papers clearly showed this, but he had been buried under a provisional wooden cross with his name inaccurately spelled. His body was recovered for proper identification and the surname was corrected on the cross.

It was not until 12 June 1940 that Johan's wife was notified officially of her husband's death. Killed in action, as she had feared all along. The next day, 13 June, her new-born son also died. She herself died in 1944, leaving no children. Johan's body was buried almost where he had been found, now a front row of the Grebbeberg National War Cemetery. Proper tombstones engraved with Dutch soldier's names replaced the wooden crosses only after the war. The graveyard of 1940 became the Grebbeberg National War Cemetery in 1955.

Germans buried there in 1940, 165 men in all, were exhumed after 1945, removed from the Grebbeberg and reburied in an exclusive remote field near IJsselstein, a village in the province of Brabant. It is reserved for German soldiers only, killed in action in the Netherlands in the Second World War, unless their descendants preferred to have them buried in Germany. The Dutch have not been keen on the Germans being buried together with their own dead in the Grebbeberg, the Arnhem area or anywhere else. Germans killed in action are not commemorated in the Netherlands in any way. The same thing happened at Arnhem and Oosterbeek after Market Garden. While British, Polish and other soldiers of the Battle of Arnhem are put to rest in the same cemetery, all German dead were exhumed and removed to Brabant in 1945 or soon after.

Johan Kuiper's surviving family-members received a posthumous bronze medal in 1948 for his part in 'unusual military operations', a consolation prize from a state that had

Bronze cross awarded to Johan Kuiper, who was killed in action on 13 May 1940. He was one of 3,511 Dutch, British, Canadian, American and Polish soldiers to receive the award for bravery, which was instituted by Queeen Wilhelmina on 11 June 1940.

German lightly armoured train derailed beyond Gennep, after having hit dragon's teeth (the pointed bars between the wrecked locomotive and the two Germans) on 10 May 1940. The speeding train has been thrown off the track. The sunlight on the dragon's teeth shows that the train was coming from the east. The signal post reads 'stop'.

lacked the political guts of taking sides in time. Most of those slaughtered at the Grebbeberg were killed in an area only about 2 kilometres square. This paints a picture of how fierce the fighting was. As far as the Dutch were concerned, the number of those killed was almost one quarter of the total number killed in action during the German invasion in 1940. Obviously, these figures are very small compared with other loss of human life in the two World Wars. People here are well aware of such huge differences, but to us, every death was important.

The outcome of the battle was dreadful for the defenders, as it confirmed what the Dutch people had believed for years; their army was incapable of defending their own country when attacked from the east. This was not altogether fair, of course, when comparing the size of the Dutch population and force with the Germans' which was about ten times larger and much more industrialized. There was no reason to compare the Dutch with David, when he faced Goliath, but the Dutch felt they faced defeat in a matter of days. For Hitler's self-confident, war-oriented forces the result was as successful as they had foreseen. They were sure that more victories lay ahead.

Chapter Six

A Palace Too Far

Queen Wilhelmina of the Netherlands was a steadfast, energetic woman. Winston Churchill called her 'the only man in the Dutch cabinet', when she was in exile in London. She called Hitler 'the arch-enemy of mankind'. When war broke out she was 59 years of age and had been on the throne since she was 18 and a widow since 1934. Although she had been informed secretly that she and the Dutch cabinet were to be arrested on the day of a German invasion, the Queen refused to leave the country on 10 May or the days afterwards.

As head of state, Queen Wilhelmina was always very much involved in state affairs, both before and during the war. She advocated strong armed forces, but in accordance with prevailing democratic rules, her direct power was limited. Following Germany's aggression in Czechoslovakia, Poland and Scandinavia, Wilhelmina fully shared the general Dutch opinion that Germans could no longer be seen as friendly Europeans from a neighbouring country. Throughout the war, from London and in fact until she died in 1962, Wilhelmina remained irreconcilable towards Germany; Nazis in particular, of course, as well as Dutch political weaklings who were prepared to bend and live with Hitler's regime. One of those was a cabinet member!

The Queen and her family, that is Crown Princess Juliana, her husband and two children, Princesses Beatrix and Irene, were in her residential palace just outside The Hague on 10 May 1940. At 3.30 in the morning, General HQ woke her to say that a German assault of the Netherlands was imminent. The royals had spent the night in the palace's underground shelter. The Queen woke Princess Juliana, saying, *'Ze zijn er,'* ('They are here'). At about nine o'clock that morning, the Queen moved to her business palace in Noordeinde, a street in the centre of The Hague. They discussed whether the Crown Princess, Wilhelmina's only child, should take her family to England. But on 10 May, the streets of The Hague were in uproar and it was considered too dangerous to travel. Conditions were worse the next day and Queen Wilhelmina decided that she and her children would not leave The Hague.

An hour after her arrival at Noordeinde, Queen Wilhelmina addressed the Dutch people by radio with remarkably strong words. 'I herewith point a fiery protest at this shameless and infamous violation of good faith and invasion of what is decent among civilised states.' She urged the Dutch people to take up arms and present resistance when she added, 'I and my government will now do our duties. You do yours…' Odd as it may sound, 'fiery protest' is a direct translation of her words here, '*vlammend protest*'. They were clear to anyone, although it wasn't regular Dutch either. The Dutch government officially declared war on Germany the same morning. It was a reply to the strange German statement earlier that morning. The Germans were just invading another neighbouring country, for a second time since 1914, though admittedly not the same ones. Queen Wilhelmina's strongly worded message was well understood in Berlin.

The impending departure of the Queen and cabinet was discussed in a meeting later in the morning. According to the Dutch Constitution, the 'seat of the government' (head of state and cabinet) could 'not be outside the Netherlands'. Clearly this was a big problem, because it was certainly unwise for the queen to stay. But Wilhelmina did not want to go to the Dutch East Indies, which she believed were too hot. For the same reasons she may have rejected Suriname or the Netherlands Antilles. This violation of neutrality, this sudden situation of war and occupation was an emergency not provided for in the Constitution of the Netherlands. Certain arrangements had been made, however, with the British government, including King George VI personally, in case of a German attack on the Netherlands. They were mentioned in a statement by Prime Minister Neville Chamberlain on 18 April 1939, when he declared that Britain was to come to the aid of 'Holland', Denmark and Switzerland in the case of a German attack.

The statement followed a pact of mutual assistance between Britain, France and Poland in the case of a German attack. Yet, when small German paratroop units managed to reach the inner city of The Hague on 10 May and got quite close to crucial locations, Wilhelmina refused to leave. The Germans were now only a short distance from Binnenhof, Court of

Parliament, including the Cabinet's foremost meeting room. Exchanges of fire took place at a major junction just a 100m (300ft) from there. At that moment, the royal palace was less than 500m (1700ft) away, as was General HQ. The Queen, cabinet members and those at General HQ may have heard the shooting in the streets, but the Germans did not really come close to the royal palace or HQs. Skirmishes between German soldiers and local constables also took place in at least two more places in city. These Germans had entered the city either from Ockenburg or from the beach.

Even so, the Germans did not succeed in advancing to the royal palace. Members of the cabinet repeatedly urged the Queen to leave, but she stayed put. As ordered by Hitler, the Queen was to announce surrender of the Dutch forces to the Germans immediately in a signed document and also a broadcast by radio. Next, she was to be taken to Germany as a prisoner. It is obvious that Hitler expected a Dutch surrender and was after total humiliation of the Queen and the Dutch population on the day of invasion.

By 12 May, Wilhelmina ordered Juliana and her family to leave the country. Juliana may not have liked the idea of her mother staying behind, but the Queen decided to stay in The Hague as long as possible. The royal family was small, only five in all spread over three generations, but as a first family they all stood out and can be considered to be among the first refugees to escape from the Netherlands in 1940. Juliana's family was taken to Ijmuiden harbour on the North Sea, west of Amsterdam. They travelled to Ijmuiden in an armoured truck belonging to The Netherlands Bank. A British submarine then took them to the destroyer HMS *Codrington*, waiting for them off the Dutch coast. They landed in Harwich on the same evening. A month later, at the beginning of the Battle of Britain, Princess Juliana and her daughters moved to Ottawa, Canada where they stayed for much of the war and where a third daughter, Princess Margriet, was born.

Two Dutch ministers, including the foreign minister, and a few officials had headed for London on 10 May in a plane. They negotiated with Churchill on 12 May, requesting military assistance on behalf of their beleaguered forces. Obviously, this would mean large-scale assistance. This request put the Dutch definitively on the British side of the conflict, later the Allied side, from their previous position of neutrality. The request was news, but not a surprise. In previous months Belgian, French and British government officials had negotiated how to come to the rescue if the poorly prepared Netherlands were to be attacked.

British Army expeditionary forces had been present in France of course since 1939 and British forces were supposed to keep the Germans out of Scandinavia. On 10 May a detachment of British Royal Engineers arrived at the Hook of Holland, this time following a British proposal. The British had suggested destruction of large oil supplies in the hands of BP in the harbour of Rotterdam, following the German assault of the city. The idea behind this was to prevent these stocks being used in an assault on the British mainland by the Germans. On Monday 13th, British and Dutch forces blew up these oil supplies and all refinery equipment at Pernis near Rotterdam, with RAF back-up.

An important measure was proclaimed by the Dutch government on 12 May, when all civil maritime officers and crew were declared conscripts and ordered to secure all sea-going vessels beyond control of the enemy. This meant 'sail to British harbours' if near the Netherlands or Britain. An order of this kind was understood very quickly, of course, and resulted in safeguarding 2,5 millions of tons of cargo from falling into German hands. A German counter-order was ignored.

A small British military force set out for the Hook of Holland on the same day. This Harpoon Force, as it was code-named, was commanded by Lieutenant Colonel Joseph Haydon, and was 'to advance to The Hague and to cooperate with the local authorities and troops in order to repair the situation and to safeguard the Dutch government.' The Army units were to 'comply with requests of Dutch governments' unless Haydon considered the lives of his 650-strong battalion to be in extreme danger. Harpoon Force included Royal Navy destroyer HMS *Hereward* and two more Royal Navy vessels, HMS *Venomous* and HMS *Verity*.

They were at anchor off the Hook of Holland, which was less than 20km (12 miles) from the Noordeinde Palace and were ready to take the Queen and her cabinet into exile. The ships were to take British diplomats and civilians from Belgium as well. Among the first to embark were three RAF-men who had had a share in bombing Rotterdam-Waalhaven on 11 May.

Members of the cabinet urged the Queen to leave the country once again on 12 May. It is reported that she set little value on the opinion of the cabinet or individual members; she certainly ignored their suggestions at first, but she changed her mind in the course of the day. On 13 May at 4am (just three in the morning in London) she made an emergency phone call to George VI. She announced that she would arrive as agreed. In a cabinet meeting early the following morning in which Winkelman took part as Supreme Commander, she was urged to set out for London. He made it clear that most Dutch forces were nearing the end of their facilities. German tanks had been reported to be near Rotterdam, a mere 35km (22 miles) from The Hague. Also, German airborne forces were still at large in and around The Hague and there was a great risk to her safety.

Queen Wilhelmina accepted the general's words. Reluctantly she and all remaining members of the cabinet prepared for leaving the Netherlands within a few hours. Following the queen's departure from the country, Winkelman became the highest non-elected authority in the Netherlands in her name. Along with the cabinet, a force of about 200 military police left the Netherlands at the same time. Meanwhile, small German vessels, presumably *Schnellboote* or armed speed boats, navigated off the Dutch coast to make sure that no British amphibian landings were spotted as the Germans always feared. During this sweep, Harpoon Force and a few more British ships caught the Germans' attention and they launched an air attack but, surprisingly, they did little harm.

Even on board, Queen Wilhelmina reconsidered her decision. Instead of leaving the Netherlands entirely, she asked that they take her to the city of Breskens, Zeeland-Flanders opposite Vlissingen, as this was in Dutch hands still. Her model was Belgian King Albert I during the First World War, who had remained in Belgium's own Westhook for most of 1914 and after, rather than moving to nearby France, therefore sending a clear message that in 1914, the German Army had not been able to conquer all of Belgium. King Albert was a shining example to Wilhelmina in 1940, until she learned that Breskens was being bombed by the Luftwaffe. Only then did she agree to set out for Britain, which was finally proved to her to be the best decision. In the evening Queen Wilhelmina was seen by King George VI at Buckingham palace, where she was officially told that Britain was ready to take the Queen and cabinet into exile.

Hitler may well have gnashed his teeth when it was reported that Queen Wilhelmina and the entire Dutch cabinet had slipped away. Instead, the Queen had escaped, several thousands of German soldiers had been sent to Britain as POWs and the fighting continued. The city of Rotterdam was still not in German hands despite four days of fighting and bombing. The Hague and Noordeinde palace definitely was a palace too far. What a costly operation it was, at the loss of so many men and so much equipment, to establish not a single meaningful result. Hitler and Goering considered more plans to bring the Dutch to their knees, whatever the cost might be.

Queen Wilhelmina continued to act as Head of State whenever possible throughout the war. Her strong character dominated most members of the Dutch cabinet. But she struggled with the rather weak attitude of some cabinet members. One of those was Prime Minister Dirk Jan de Geer, who

Queen Wilhelmina frequently addressed the Dutch population by radio from London. From 28 July 1940 onwards, the BBC granted daily air time to 'Radio Oranje', which kept those at home aware of how the war was progressing in the Netherlands and the Dutch Indies. Listening to foreign radio was forbidden by the Nazis in Germany and in all occupied countries.

was with her in London. De Geer declared publicly in August 1940 that Britain could never win the war and concluded that a peace treaty with Germany was inevitable. The Queen therefore considered him a coward and fired him. He then escaped to the Netherlands without having consulted the Queen and had wanted to speak to Hitler. This was unsuccessful and de Geer was convicted of treason after the war.

He was succeeded in London by Pieter S. Gerbrandy, a most self-willed Frisian, a lawyer and a professor of law before being a cabinet member. He had to learn English after his sudden arrival in London. Churchill is said to have nicknamed him Mr. Sherrybrandy. One day, Mr. Gerbrandy entered Churchill's office and greeted him by saying, 'Good-bye, Mr. Churchill!' Afterwards, Churchill said said: 'That was the shortest conversation I've ever had.' Gerbrandy was doing his best, but in Dutch and under very familiar circumstances only, hello and good-bye are the same word.

Whilst in Britain, Queen Wilhelmina's first place of residence was 82 Eaton Square in Belgravia. However, she preferred a more modest lifestyle and moved to Roe Cottage, Priory Lane, Roehampton, now overlooking the Golf Club. German air raids over London forced her to move further out of London, to Stubbings House in Bisham, Berkshire, still only 57km (39 miles) from London, where she stayed until early 1944. For some reason, she then moved to South Mimms, Hertfordshire, which is about 20km (12 miles) north of London. But here, she was almost hit by a Luftwaffe bomb which exploded only a few feet from her house, killing two Dutch military policemen who were standing guard. Because of the damage to the house, the Queen moved back to Stubbings House first and then to Laneswood, in the village of Mortimer near Reading. She returned to the Netherlands for good on 3 May 1945.

Chapter Seven

Inevitable Surrender

I t was clear to the High Command that the country was no longer in their hands. There were two small exceptions. One was at the IJsselmeer Closure Dike in the north, where the Dutch Army and Navy, had resisted all German attacks. The second was Zeeland province, where no sizable German forces had advanced yet and where both Dutch and French forces were prepared to face them. Neither could hold out for long.

The German threat that four major cities were 'to share the same fate' as Rotterdam, which had been extensively bombed, 'in case your chief-commander will not surrender', was good enough for Winkelman to act as the Germans required. Giving in, in this uneven warfare, and avoid more atrocious air attacks, proved the best choice and he ordered all army and navy troops in the country to cease fire late in the afternoon of 14 May.

Very early the next day, General Winkelman and his staff made their way from The Hague to a small school at Rysoord. The heart of Rotterdam, the 'safest place in the country', as he could see for himself, was smoking and burning. In his company were Lieutenant General Arnhem Baron van Voorst tot Voorst, Lieutenant Commander D.G. van Doorninck as an aide-de-camp to represent the Royal (Dutch) Navy and a general staff captain, J.D. Schepers. At Rysoord they met the German delegation of five men. Their interpreter again was Dutch-speaking Austrian Dr Plutzar.

Negotiations with the Germans took almost two hours. Winkelman managed to exclude the remaining Dutch forces in Zeeland from capitulation, well aware that this achievement was little more than a stay of execution. It was also agreed that any Dutch military who had escaped to Great Britain, were excluded from the surrender. Yet they were ordered by Hitler, by radio, to return to the Netherlands; his orders were ignored. Winkelman, who held the highest authority in the Netherlands until the Dutch surrender, told the Germans, 'We do not conclude a peace treaty, we will continue the war.' Any German comments are not registered. Maybe this was his answer to the German invitation if there was anything left to say.

The Dutch capitulation, one of the most regrettable moments in the country's history, was made public by radio at 8.30 on the evening of 15 May. German troops entered Amsterdam and The Hague the next day and the occupation became effective all over the country shortly after. The occupation of the Netherlands south of the rivers lasted four years and four months, until 17 September 1944. In Zeeland it took a few more months. North of the rivers it lasted for the next five years and all but ten days. The area between the rivers was a battle ground until late April and early May 1945, except when it was inundated.

'A people neglecting its defence, puts its freedom at stake,' or, in Dutch, *'Een volk dat zijn verdediging verwaarloost, zet zijn vrijheid op het spel'*. This uneasy truth, this motto, now sits at the entrance to the Rysoord school which has become a modest Second World War museum. Even today, it is a very serious, worthwhile admonition to the Dutch and a small commemoration of the Dutch capitulation of 1940. The Dutch generation of the early twenties which had tucked away this truth, were presented with an expensive bill from 1940 to 1945 and many years after. But it was a modest bill as well, in the sense that others were to take up the real effort of liberating the Dutch and paid a second bill with many lives.

The five days-war cost the lives of 2,332 Dutch soldiers and citizens, as well as about 2,500 Germans, with 700 Germans missing. There were 6,000 wounded on the Dutch side, 5,500 among the Germans. The Dutch had taken 2,000 POWs of which more than half were transported to Britain and later to Canada. The Germans, before and after the surrender, took 271,668 Dutch POWs without great effort. Many of those were released a few weeks later. Officers were held in captivity longer.

At a later stage, the Germans summoned all former officers to report to various places. A few did not trust the Germans and went into hiding. Those who followed this order were taken prisoner and sent to Stalags, German POW camps. In addition, the Germans seized many prominent pre-war politicians who were either interned in a special camp in the Netherlands, or taken to Germany.

Two Dutch officers, General Henri Winkelman (centre) and Lieutenant General Herman van Voorst tot Voorst (right) leaving the school at Rysoord after having signed the Dutch surrender on 15 May 1940, at 10.15 am. Look at the uneasy way both men hold their hands. The German on the far left is a member of the *Feldgendarmerie* or Military Police. No press appear to be present to ask the generals any relevant questions.

Troops in Zeeland province on the Walchderen peninsula and in Zeeland-Flanders (which borders Belgium), opposite the Wester-Scheldt from Vlissingen and the south-westernmost part of the Netherlands, were excluded from this capitulation. The situation at Walcheren, where the small city of Middelburg is provincial capital, was unusual. Dutch forces were joined by French army units on 10 May voluntarily – the French arrived without prior notice. Their presence and share in the defence were welcomed, but rather useless. But while the Dutch forces were commanded by a rear-admiral who reported to General Winkelman, French forces were commanded by an infantry general who reported to the French supreme command in Paris. To make things somewhat more complicated, in 1940 there was quite a language barrier between the Dutch and the French.

The French primarily intended to protect and defend the mouth of the Wester-Scheldt, the estuary between Vlissingen and Zeeland-Flanders. This is the marine entrance to Antwerp. The north banks are Walcheren, one neighbouring peninsula, South-Beveland, and a connecting dam in between. This dam was 800m (2,700ft) long. German troops attacked South-Beveland and the city of Goes on 15 May. They reached the western end of the peninsula and Zeeland-Flanders a few days later which completed the German occupation of the Netherlands.

Nazi-rulers took over. While Belgium was to be subjected to a military government, the Dutch were primarily ruled by two SS men from 1940 to 1945. The Dutch Parliament was no longer in place following its formal closing session on 10 May, which was 'confirmed' by the Germans on 22 June and no elections were to be held. These and the traditional Dutch freedoms of thinking, speaking, publishing, doing and going were swept away like autumn leaves. The number one Nazi in the Netherlands was Dr Arthur Seyss-Inquart. Born in Moravia, he was the former Austrian Minister of the Interior. In 1938, he had betrayed a large part of the Austrian population which enabled Hitler to enact the *Anschluss*, Hitler's annexation of Austria. He acted as a governor in the true sense.

Seyss-Inquart became *Reichskommisar für den besetzten Niederlanden* – the Reichscommissioner, Hitler's governor, of the occupied Netherlands. Basically, Hitler wanted the Netherlands to become part of his greater Germanic Empire, as this backward Austrian nationalist considered the Dutch as fellow members of the so-called Aryan super race. Seyss-Inquart, who as a *Reichsminister* reported to Hitler directly, cooperated with another Austrian, Hanns Albin Rauter.

Rauter became SD and Gestapo police chief in the Netherlands. As an SS member, he was a *Obergruppenführer*. The word Gestapo was short for (German) Secret State Police. In rank and as an executioner, Rauter was called 'the most bloodthirsty chieftain of the German police in the Netherlands' in 1945. As an *Obergruppenführer*, he became a full equivalent of Adolf Eichmann who played a major role in the holocaust, and Reinhard Heydrich in Czechoslovakia, who was assassinated in 1942. Both were foremost, ruthless personifications of Nazism.

The SD, which in the Netherlands was very well organized, operated closely with other German police forces, such as the *Kripo,* short for criminal police. In the Nazi era yet another SS branch was in force, the *Sicherheitsdienst* (Security Service). The SD was a security service of the SS, in part acting as a political police. Rauter's titles and ranks in the SS and his field of operation were long and complicated; his ranks in the Netherlands were SS equivalents of all ranks of an army general.

The two men exerted an unprecedented reign of terror in the Netherlands. They were accountable for the deportation of politicians, Resistance fighters and all Jewish and Romany citizens in the Netherlands. They had them deported to the concentration camps in Germany and the extermination camps in Poland, thereby cashing in their properties on behalf of the German treasury, as they were sure these victims would never return. They were responsible for ordering and allowing unlimited imprisonment without charges in the Netherlands, torturing and shooting of Resistance fighters and systematic looting. In fact, both men were the eyes, ears and hands of Adolf Hitler, the boots and means of torture of Heinrich Himmler and their reign of Nazi terror in the country until their very last days in service.

As one of the two foremost Nazi-scourges in the Netherlands, Austrian *Reichsminister* and *Reichskommissar* Arthur Seyss-Inquart was tried in the first sitting of the Nuremberg Trials. He was found guilty of planning, initiating and waging wars of aggression in Poland and the Netherlands respectively, of crimes against humanity including the deportation and expulsion of at least a 102,000 Dutch Jewish residents killed (out of a total of 140,000 in 1940). He was also found guilty of the execution of resistance members and the granting of permission to hang prominent Dutch citizens as acts of revenge. Seyss-Inquart was hanged in Nuremberg in October, 1946.

Being the highest SS chief in the Netherlands, Lieutenant General Hanns Rauter reported directly to Himmler, the *Reichsfüehrer SS,* and then to Seyss-Inquart. Rauter was the more ruthless of the two throughout the war. He is considered a typical agent of the merciless anti-Jew of the twenties in Austria and Germany. Rauter was also responsible for the deportation of all Jewish civilians in the Netherlands (of which 1,300 came from Arnhem alone), round-ups of 500,000 men 18 years of age and up, to be deported to German industries as replacements for Germans drafted into the military,

Arrival of a trainload of Jewish citizens from Hungary at Auschwitz extermination camp. Families have just been separated and people are selected as potential workers (the column of men on the right), while all those on the left – elderly, women, children, the sick – are to be gassed immediately. Only the SS men and the inmates in their striped uniforms knew what lay ahead within the next hour.

detection, imprisonment and often execution of resistance fighters and exercise of the Nazi terror in the Netherlands.

Rauter's main Gestapo office was in The Hague. A branch office of Rauter's Gestapo, one of only a few in the country, was in a rural estate within the city of Arnhem, close to the mansion Rauter had confiscated for himself. There was a second SS office in Arnhem. Here, the SD was in office. It gained a very infamous reputation in the city and the area. Throughout the years of war, so many citizens of Arnhem and elsewhere were tortured and interrogated there, that Arnhem's city management gave the house (Utrechtseweg 55-A) a different number after the war. A bronze plate against the wall however acts as a reminder of the horrifying experiences of many Dutch citizens inside this war-time office.

General Winkelman was not taken into German custody on or after 15 May, but he did fall victim to typical German small-mindedness over a month later. As a young student in Germany, Prince Bernhard of Lippe-Biesterfeld used to wear a white carnation in a button-hole as a personal trade-mark. The Prince maintained this habit when he married Princess Juliana of the Netherlands in 1937, and clearly choose the side of the Dutch when hostilities broke out. The Prince's birthday was 29 June, and was the first royal birthday after the capitulation.

The Dutch give much attention to anniversaries of relatives, friends and neighbours. Anniversaries are cheerful social events. Within family circles, birthdays are a reason to get together, both relatives and friends, from nearby and from other places. The 'lucky duck' will receive presents, even more than on Sinterklaas' birthday, 5 December. 'When do you celebrate your birthday?' is a common question in social life. Phone calls and emails are made to congratulate, postcards are written (sometimes even between divorced people) and during birthday parties, preferably on the day of birth, everybody present is congratulated by shaking hands and giving kisses. Non-Dutch people when invited are often amazed and ask: 'Do all these people have their birthday?' So, small wonder that Prince Bernhard's birthday was a stimulus this time to celebrate his anniversary with cheers and in public. And with a carnation.

Dutch flags were waved from many houses and all church towers all over the Netherlands and the National Anthem was sung in the streets. Flags waving was usual. Singing the National Anthem was an expression of protest, this time. In The Hague, at Noordeinde palace, as well as several other places in the country, open gatherings took place where people wore white carnations in their button-holes or pinned to their dresses, all in honour of Prince Berhnard's birthday. General Winkelman was one of those who participated in the demonstrations.

At the Noordeinde palace, a book of congratulations was being signed by visitors. General Winkelman, a private citizen now, was one of the first to sign. Flowers were laid by other visitors in front of the palace – all to show their disgust at the German occupation. As a former, short-lived representative of the Queen, Winkelman declared that he refused to cooperate with the Germans. He made clear that Dutch enterprises, civil servants and individual workers should not accept or carry out Nazi-orders.

The scale of this clear anti-German demonstration was an unpleasant surprise to the Germans. Sometimes surprisingly politically naïve, they believed themselves popular or at least acceptable with the Dutch. Well, they were not. And as it happened, Dr. Joseph Goebbels, Hitler's Minister of Propaganda, visited The Hague by chance on that first Carnation Day (*Anjerdag*). He witnessed various expressions of vociferous anti-German feelings from a window just around a corner from Noordeinde palace. Single-minded, Goebbels was outraged and ordered counter-measures with immediate effect. Even so, the white carnation quickly became a symbol of protest during the war.

In the early morning of 2 July 1940 the Germans knocked at the door of Winkelman's private house at Wassenaar and arrested him, for 'wearing a white carnation'. This arrest was a typical example of Nazi style. Was there a law that forbade wearing a white carnation? Not at all, of course, but this was a token of the new and so-called *Führer-Prinzip*, application of whatever restriction of which it was believed that Hitler might have come up with. Winkelman was put on a transport to Germany, where he was held captive throughout the war. He was not released until 12 May 1945. For wearing a carnation? A series of counter-measures was announced shortly after Goebbels' visit and the exhibition of flags and white carnations.

After Winkelman's arrest, the mayor of The Hague was fired by the Nazis because of the incident and the carnations, even though he had been a close but secret collaborator of the Gestapo since 1935. Dutch flags were banned from then onwards and they were always waved extensively on Queen's Day; Wilhelmina's was 31 August. Streets and so on named after royals were to be given different names, Goebbels ordered, while the names of these persons were no longer to be mentioned in the papers or on radio.

German propaganda images. Wehrmacht (top) and SS (below) soldiers enter Amsterdam on 16 May 1940. In the above image, Dam Square can be seen in the back-ground, while the bottom image shows Berlage Amstel bridge, one of the city's entry points. Although spectators are seen greeting the German occupiers with the Nazi salute, a large majority of the Dutch despised the Germans.

Chapter Eight

Boots of Terror

While the British at home suffered seriously from German attacks from the air and on the high seas, the Dutch suffered most from the Nazi terror, particularly the SS and their branches – just like those in all other German-occupied countries. Like millions of others on the continent, the Dutch felt the boots of terror which the British, fortunately, did not even hear. The hard sound of German boots in a street was the much feared sound of their terror. This is a major difference between the British and the Dutch experience of the war and because of this difference, the British can happily ridicule the Germans of the Second World War; the Dutch cannot and anyone who tried would be ignored.

Many Germans who were posted to the Netherlands liked living in Arnhem. There were civil servants, Army, Luftwaffe and SS officers who were all billeted in one of the barracks within the city or at Ede, or at the nearby air base at Deelen – but Arnhem was their favourite place to live. In fact, so popular was it that a large number of private houses were taken over by German families. This usually included all furniture and other household belongings as the Germans had left their own back home in Germany. The original Dutch occupants were expelled against their will, usually at short notice, and had to find accommodation elsewhere, usually with relatives in the first instance. Germans seemed to consider the Netherlands as some sort of colony. This even included all the animals of Burger's, Arnhem's city zoo.

Giving shelter to expelled families for an unknown span of time was called 'living in'. It required a great deal of willingness to please from both parties, relatives or others, be they neighbours or friends or just complete strangers, taken in as refugees. Many houses were cramped, leaving less space while requiring more tolerance and acceptance from the owners; a difficult situation for everyone. There was more 'living in' as the war progressed and even more so after Market Garden. Cramped housing and 'living in' continued for many years after the war, as housing shortages affected the Netherlands very much, just like most countries after the war.

This was different in the beginning. In an illustrated book about the fate of Arnhem during the war, called *Arnhems Kruisweg* (Arnhem's Way of the Cross), published in 1946, it reads:

'The Germans considered Arnhem as a Rhineland city, a German city, more than any other place in the Netherlands. Unprecedented numbers of Germans settled there during the occupation and they took their families with them. High ranking German civil servants who had their offices in the west of the country, lived in Arnhem. Not a single house against the steep pushed moraines, not a villa in the surrounding woods was safe. Local families just were turned out onto the streets and the Germans moved in. In Arnhem's beautiful outskirts more and more Arnhemers had to make room for Germans'.

To view things with both feet on the ground, Arnhem's beautiful outskirts are to be compared with other Dutch landscapes only; Arnhem certainly cannot be said to outperform landscapes like western Scotland or Yorkshire, for example.

Interestingly, one of the three authors of the book about Arnhem was also actively involved in informing the Allies, specifically Montgomery's HQ, about the presence of Wehrmacht and SS units in the Arnhem area, prior to Market Garden. German units, mainly battered tank forces, had settled a little north of Arnhem in the main. Similar units were 35km (21 miles) to the east. Unfortunately, this vital information was put aside in Montgomery's field truck, in his drive to materialize an outstanding military achievement. I recall having seen some of these tanks from nearby myself when they rolled down the lower end of our street during Market Garden in 1944; they were sandy-coloured as I remember. This was a change. Other German tanks and armoured cars I had seen were green, mainly.

I joined mankind, so to say, in a quiet street to the east of Arnhem. My parents lived in a detached house dating from about 1910 on a broad, slightly inclined street, lined with double rows of beech trees, for horse riders, and still today retaining the paving stones it had long before the war. The special horse-track is long gone. The quiet of this street still prevails, though some of the old beeches were taken out to make room for some cluttered car parking. After 1950, vibrant and social Amsterdam was a welcome home for me, then later The Hague and Rotterdam. The atmosphere of provincial Arnhem no longer suited me.

After my father's release by the Germans, my parents lived reasonably well at the beginning of the war, under the 'New Order', in spite of the restricting war conditions. They felt very much at ease in our street, and loved the woods and inclines quite close to our house and the undulating countryside, and so did I. That was unless the peaceful silence was suddenly interrupted, however, by frenzied dogfights, engine roaring and loud bangs in the air. They were most fearful surprises, while bullets or shrapnel could hit you anywhere. In the open, no one was safe. I could share their feelings when growing up somewhat. They were good friends with some of their Dutch neighbours, which is more important. The few German officers and their families who lived in confiscated, isolated houses in our street were ignored.

Our Dutch neighbours on one side owned a cocker spaniel who did not take to me. The spaniel may well have read the book *How to Bring Down a Small Boy*, as he bit me on the ear one day! Other dogs, perhaps with a better instinct, preferred to hate German uniforms. One small brown mutt barked at every man in a German uniform, which incorrectly included the Dutch postman. One day one of the Germans in our street got fed up with this mutt and its unvarying yapping. The man took his pistol and shot the dog, just a few metres in front of me. That was really shocking; the dog screamed miserably, then died. Two neighbouring girls, sisters Alice and Jackie Muusse, three-quarters of a century later recalled the same yapper and the same shooting.

While I was free to play in the street and among the beeches at the age of four, I was strictly forbidden to go far down or up the street and turn around the corners. Sometimes this was really challenging, as the road down our street was an arterial road with trucks and a private car now and then. More important for me were the city trams, cream coloured or partly green, leased from another company, which I loved to watch and to ride, mostly because of the sonorous humming of the electric motors or when they exerted their priority rights by ringing their bells. It was a sound that allowed no objection, at least in my small perception. To me, both sounds were as stately as the city trams themselves.

Gestapo chief Hanns Rauter's main office was in The Hague and a branch office was in a rural estate within the city of Arnhem. It was close to the mansion that the SS chief had confiscated on behalf of himself and his family. The large mansion stood at the corner of the next block from our street and this, of course, was the main reason why I was strictly forbidden to go around the corner at the end of our own street. Rauter's house was well guarded by Germans and a special basement was made to protect him, his family-members and a few more. His rank as an SS general, his Nazi-style entourage and his merciless SS aura were good enough to make me be very careful and avoid any contacts.

Alice, who lived next to us, remembers Rauter's house as well, but she also recalls something that was told to her after the war only. It is that the neighbours, the ones with the dog that bit me, gave well-concealed shelter to a small Jewish family. During the war, it was common practice that certain things were not told to small children, for fear of it reaching wrong ears. As far as I was concerned, keeping silence, hiding facts, was not usual, as I was told and had explained to me everything I asked my parents, or did not even ask. But what if Rauter or Germans living in our street were informed about the presence of concealed Jewish residents in some way? Of course, these men and women never made it to the street.

One day, an exception was made. This was 5 December 1943, when a very old Dutch (and Flemish) tradition is celebrated; a live visit by *Sinterklaas* on his so-called birthday. Saint Nicholas, the 'Spanish bishop' is an all-time friend of all children. On this birthday – which is believed to be the anniversary of his real death in the fourth century – children and even adults are given presents, like on Boxing Day and on their birthdays. Just like Santa Claus, any man can be dressed up as a *Sinterklaas* and does not need to be a Roman Catholic. Even more exceptional, the real Saint Nicholas was not from Spain as it is always said. He was a Turkish bishop, now buried in Italy.

The man is dressed in some fancy Roman Catholic bishop's attire, usually wearing a long white beard from ear to ear and is accompanied by Black Piet, his servant – a young lady usually, her face painted black. But the impressive man in this particular case was not *Sinterklaas*, as was told to Alice after the war, when children stopped believing that *Sinterklaas* really exists. In 1943, he was the Jewish citizen who was sheltered by our other neighbours. Being dressed like *Sinterklaas* was a nice and exceptional opportunity for him to be in a street for a while, without a risk of being recognized by a German as a Jewish Dutchman.

The Nazis preferred Austrians for merciless special assignments and police-work in the SS, as Austrians were even more experienced in tracking down, interrogating and torturing suspects. This difference resulted from police practices in the imperial Habsburg era, when it was a public secret

'The New Order', the title of a grim cartoon first published in an Amsterdam weekly in 1942. From right to left: a German Wehrmacht soldier in his black boots as the occupier of Dutch soil (shown by the arable land, typical haystack and windmill). Behind him are 'Betrayal' (*Verraad*, carrying a Gestapo file), 'Terror' (*Terreur*), 'Misery' (*Ellende*) and finally a diminutive and ridiculed hanger on. This was Anton Mussert, the leader of the Dutch National-Socialist Movement, NSB. The Dutch words are such that several Germans could read them without great difficulty.

that at times, people had disappeared for good once they had been taken into certain police stations in Vienna. Austrian author Franz Grillparzer was one dramatist who wrote about this in the early nineteenth century. In Germany, certain police practices like torturing were abolished as impractical and inhumane by the Prussian King, Frederick the Great in the eighteenth century. Until 1918 in Alsace-Lorraine, however, the German police and army were despised because of their way of rounding up citizens, who felt they were French.

It was also up to the Gestapo to find out what was the best time to arrest someone. They found out it was best around 5.30am, as most people are in the deepest of their sleep then and offer the least resistance when raided at home. This became the Gestapo's practice in Nazi Germany, which they extended to their jails, for interrogation, when their suspects had been arrested before. From 1939 onwards, when German troops had taken over Memel Land, the Czech part of Czechoslovakia and Poland, arrests at dawn were used in these countries as well, like in the ones occupied later.

Consequently, this included the Netherlands where, as older policemen have confirmed to me many years ago, arrests at home were not made at dawn before the Second World War. Most police forces in formerly occupied countries have abolished this contemptible practice after their countries were liberated. In a few countries, this Gestapo practice was maintained however and the Netherlands is one of countries, even to this day. Today's candidates for early-morning arrests are far less docile and more than once these attempts to arrest result in shootings. In many cases, suspects are killed by the police before they can be interrogated and tried. Has anyone ever heard a Dutch judge protest these Nazi-style arrests and subsequent state of affairs formally and publicly?

Like in most other countries occupied by the Germans – except Poland – there was a national SS force. It was established in the Netherlands from September 1940 and their black uniforms were fully in line with the Germans'. They mainly served as a reserve of the German Waffen-SS but, when needed, they were willing tools in the hands of the German SS in the Netherlands. There were about 7,000 Dutchmen in what was named Germanic SS (*Germaansche SS*) by 1942. Many of these collaborators participated on the eastern front, the Soviet Union. Those who survived and were not taken by the Soviets, were sentenced to imprisonment after the war.

One early German step was the restriction of the press, especially radio, daily newspapers and opinion magazines. Cinemas and concerts followed, the second to prevent playing 'wrong' songs. Seyss-Inquart promised not to interfere with newspapers, provided they would be 'loyal', or support the German interests. Communist and anti-fascist papers however were no longer allowed, one social-democratic paper got a national socialist as their publisher. A number of newspapers were forced to merge in 1942, 'due to paper scarcity' as it was said. The next year, a number of other papers were no longer to be published. As a few journalists who worked in those years have explained to me since, there was no preceding or restrictive German censorship of Dutch newspapers.

But if a paper had circulated news or a feature which the Germans did not want, strong criticism followed or even worse, in certain cases in connection with sanctions. This caused the revival of an old journalists' trick. Newspapers reported in such cases using the phrase, 'The authorities deny …' followed by the news that was denied by the Germans. This trick was not fit for every occasion, but to a careful and intelligent reader it was a very effective way to inform the public properly. Still another reaction was the founding of so-called underground, or illegal newspapers. Most of them started as one-page stencilled hand-outs, delivered at specific, reliable addresses. Several editors or small editorial staffs were rounded up and imprisoned. Many were shot. Four of these hand-outs have survived. Postwar, they became; a Protestant Christian daily; a general, not party-linked daily; an opinion weekly which is still with us, and one communist daily which, like the Dutch Communist Party itself, has not survived.

In 1941, the Dutch led the way in Europe with the so-called 'February Strike'. On the 25th, men employed in the harbour of Amsterdam went on strike to protest at the round-ups of young Jewish men, as well as some other anti-Jewish incidents in previous days. In the next few days these pro-Jew strikes spread to other towns. Heavy confrontations with the Germans inevitably followed. This February strike was the only public protest in Europe by non-Jews against Nazi persecution of Jewish residents. By order of Rauter and Himmler, very severe counter-measures were taken and 427

Two humiliating images of Amsterdam showing Jewish citizens being rounded up on 22 February 1941. The location, Jonas Daniël Meyerplein, is in the heart of the Jewish quarter, between Amsterdam's two main synagogues. In total, 427 citizens were deported to Buchenwald and Mauthausen concentration camps.

Jewish civilians were arrested and deported to Buchenwald and Mauthausen. Only two returned in 1945.

The February strike is still commemorated each year. The focal point is a statue called The Dockworker (to symbolise the first to strike) at a triangular place in Amsterdam between the High German or Ashkenazi synagogue of 1671 and the opposite Portuguese or Sephardic synagogue of the same era. It is the place where the Jewish citizens were driven together like cattle in 1941. Anti-German feelings still run high in Amsterdam to this day and the memories of the Nazi's conduct and the February strike are the main reasons.

The events in Amsterdam became world news very quickly, for some reason unnoticed by the German censorship. The news broke almost a year before America entered the war. Seyss-Inquart and the Germans in Amsterdam were furious about the stream of reports for a number of days. They suspected how and from where the news had left Amsterdam, but they never proved that Henk Kersting was the source of the reports. There was no contract as a token of his relationship with Associated Press who had leaked the news.

Other methods by which the Germans Nazified the Netherlands were to target two Dutch trade unions from mid-July. The Nazis took over all possessions of NVV, biggest trade union. The assumption was made that these unions were socialist, but there was never any hard evidence. The union's possessions included a roll of names and addresses of members, of course, but this was also true for any city council. The NVV board was replaced by a Dutch Nazi, who was convicted to twenty years imprisonment after the war. This, in fact, was the first major step toward Hitler's *Gleichschaltung* or equalization as executed in Germany from early 1933 onwards, when Hitler had first come to power.

No one in a position of authority in the Netherlands was a match for the brutal and violent Nazis, who simply took over by surprise and announced that from now on, they were in charge. Their abilities were unimportant; only their membership of the Nazi Party counted. Most of them were rather incompetent boors, like the last mayor of Arnhem appointed in wartime.

The Nazification meant total submission of every organization, without exceptions, to Nazi order. It involved mayors, councillors, all

The boots of terror. German propaganda image of Dutch SS in training at a barracks in Germany. The soldier in the middle seems to need a lot of support from his comrades.

larger manufacturing companies, churches, youth hostels and almost any organization of which an average European society is made up. Boy scouts packs were forbidden. Managers replaced or removed from their positions were degraded or became jobless. This also included painters and sculptors involved in the creation of abstract art, which the Nazis believed was degraded.

The constitutional right of free speech was restricted, whereas on 26 June membership of Nazi and right wing organisations became legal. This might look like a liberal step, but actually it was another example of totalitarianism. In early July, individual's capital was seized which ultimately turned against the Germans.

The first round-ups of Jewish citizens in Amsterdam was in June 1940. The next major step, and in fact the first towards the most grievous Nazi extermination of Jewish civilians and some smaller ethnic groups, was proclaimed on 1 October 1940. Jewish residents in certain positions had to sign a document in which they stated that neither they themselves, nor their parents or grandparents were Jewish citizens. If the so-called Aryan-statement was false (like a denial), they were sacked from their jobs. These people were Dutch citizens, just 'like you and me'. The existence of Aryans, the so-called superior human beings, is a fantasy of fanatics and reflected nineteenth century twisted racist thinking in Europe. It was the real beginning of all that followed against the lives and property of Jewish inhabitants of the Netherlands during the Second World War, one of the bloodiest steps of mankind against any ethnic group, Jewish or otherwise.

Next, people and their spouses with 'Jewish blood', or who were Jewish in part, no longer could be given public jobs. These resulted in the unexpected instant dismissals of Jewish public servants, university professors and staff-members on 22 November 1940. At the University of Leiden two such dismissals caused one non-Jewish professor of law, Dr Rudolph P. Cleveringa, to issue an eloquent and very sharp formulated protest against this unlawful discrimination. Professor Cleveringa was arrested immediately and kept in prison until the summer of 1941. As a protest, all those studying and employed at the University of Leiden and the Technical High School of Delft, now the technical university, went on strike for 48 hours. As a retaliation, both institutions were closed by the Germans. In early 2015, after a free poll in Leiden among the well-educated, Professor Cleveringa's speech was declared the best ever made in the Netherlands.

In cinemas, Jewish audiences were prohibited from 8 January 1941 on. Five days later, all Jews or those with Jewish ancestry were ordered to report themselves. Late in April 1942, all Jews were ordered to wear the well-known Jewish badge on their clothes, a six pointed yellow star. The Jewish quarter of Amsterdam was isolated with barbed wire. Previously, there was no ghetto in Amsterdam and Jewish residents lived all over the city, just like Anne Frank and her family, both before and during their time hiding in Prinsengracht. For this, Amsterdam traditionally was seen as the Jerusalem of the West.

The systematic deportation of Jewish citizens 'to the East', in reality to the extermination camps, began on 13 July, 1942. Almost 62,000 Jewish men, women and children from Amsterdam were exterminated by the Germans by early 1945, more than half of all murdered Dutch Jews. When I was living in Amsterdam in the fifties, a married Jewish couple lived next door to my cousins. From a family of 250 relatives some years before, they were the only two persons who had survived. All were killed in the gas chambers.

Well-known images the world over are those of Jewish people being locked up in a freight train, after which the train leaves a platform. For decades it was unclear where in Europe and when these images were taken, but it was in fact Westerbork camp in the eastern Netherlands. Consequently, it was one of those trains which took Jewish citizens of all ages to the gas chambers in Poland. These steps were followed many times, particularly against Dutch Resistance, or citizens who gave shelter to people wanted by 'the occupier', or those who had helped Allied airmen and soldiers to return to Britain. They were steps in black boots, a burden forever in German history.

Caroline Kuiper was the second in a 'sixpack' of young children at the time. She was six to eleven years old during the war, a school teacher later in life. John, her first younger brother, is nearly three years younger. They lived near the plant where her father was employed as a chief mechanic, their home separated only by a railway junction. One line leads to Germany, one to the north and parallels the IJssel River, the other to Arnhem's station. Caroline and John recall things very well.

'The freight trains left for Germany in which rounded up young men and Jewish families were packed. Those young men were forced to work in German industries. The Jewish men and women or even families with elderly people and very young children went to extermination camps, the gas chambers, most of which were in Poland. We did not really see these different kinds of people, but we knew from elder people. We experienced these trains and their forced passengers as threatening.

'Now and then we found small notes alongside the nearby railway embankment, dropped by people from those trains, in which anyone who might read it was requested to notify their next of kin in this or whatever town. Their own names and addresses were included. Usually, these people had been raided in the streets, often aware of nothing. Comparable to arrests. Just because they were Jewish citizens, or because of manpower needed in German factories. In very many situations, those at home were aware of missing family members only. Nothing they knew about whatever kind of arrest, albeit events or suspicions like those became clear very rapidly. Horrifying, is what these small notes were. And certainly because of special family names, it also became clear to us when the senders were Jewish people. Just grabbed from the streets in the later years of the war, on their way to destruction like pigs.

'These freight trains often were fired at from Allied planes. Pilots were unaware, obviously, that the freight trains carried human beings. But their bullets did not only hit the trains. We at home or in our backyards got portions of bullets as well, hitting roofs and windows. There were special directives for the trains. They were stopped in the case of air-raids, to enable engine crews and military guards to get off and take shelter. Those rounded up for work in Germany were also allowed to get off. Many of those, meanwhile, took the opportunity to escape. Jewish people were never allowed to leave the trains. They were on their way to hell anyway, so to be killed somewhat earlier did not make a difference to the Germans. However, we were told that trains carried people for German factories only, when people got off the trains. Then why had the others to stay on the same trains, or were forbidden to get off at all?'

Black boots of terror also knocked at people's front doors once possession of so-called 'wireless radio sets' was no longer allowed throughout the country, in mid-May 1943. Listening to radios, particularly non-Dutch broadcasting stations such as the BBC, had been forbidden shortly after the Germans had occupied the country. Consequently, Dutch radio broadcasts from Hilversum, the Dutch radio city, were terminated. But it was not enough, since thousands ignored the prohibition and continued listening to the radio, particularly the BBC and Radio Oranje from London. Radios were hidden in any place in a house it was thought the Germans wouldn't think of, or know how to find. My parents were among those while Jackie Muusse – Jacqueline as she called herself later – and I were allowed, sometimes, to listen to the radio. But hush! Never talk about the radio! Germans, assisted by collaborators like local police or NS men, then started to collect radio sets wherever they believed there was one.

This caused an incident in Arnhem which was followed by much merriment throughout the city, although certainly it was not the only place where an incident like this took place. As the story went, a German and a Dutch collaborator rang at someone's doorbell. They told the woman, who was living in an upstairs flat, to present her radio downstairs. They were not the small ones we are used to today, they could be the size of a laptop and some 20cm or more high. They were vulnerable technical pieces, usually in nice wooden casings. They contained special lamps and other glassware. There was no way the lady could refuse the order. 'Alright,' she shouted down the stairs, 'you will have it!' Next she opened her window and threw the radio right in front of the German and his colleague down below on the street. 'There you are!' she shouted again, and closed her window.

The size of the Dutch Resistance was by no means as impressive that which the Germans faced in France or Yugoslavia, but it was there and it cost the lives of thousands of Dutch men and women who were hunted down. Thousands of others escaped arrests, over 350,000 at its peak, and went into hiding from the Germans – either moving from towns to the province, or to other provinces, or to a different district. In a flat country like the Netherlands, it was not an easy thing. Others had tried to make their way to Britain. This caused social problems, particularly in the case of sailors' families when the sailors had escaped, leaving these families without income and rationing coupons.

To compensate for lack of a sailor's pay and that of the thousands of others who had to escape from their jobs and families, some people joined forces and carried out the biggest robbery of The Netherlands Bank even to this day. It was a total success. Families then were paid close to pre-war levels, including rationing coupons. Much more money and coupons were needed after 17 September 1944, when, because of Market Garden, a national railway strike was proclaimed by the Dutch government in London. The idea was to block all rail traffic until Market Garden could be completed, a week or so later. Unfortunately, this strike lasted until 7 May 1945. Dutch Railways, not including the employees, became part of the *Deutsche Reichsbahn*, in spite of many acts of sabotage by Dutch resistance workers.

Obviously, the German occupation cost the lives of many for an innumerable number of reasons. Hundreds or thousands of victims died in jails and prisons as a result of torture, in open fire exchanges, in front of death squads, in German industries and camps and finally, of course, on the German sides of the fronts, in the Soviet Union particularly.

The German revenge for a Dutch assault between Putten and another small municipality on 1 October 1944, is very reminiscent of the Oradour-sur-Glane massacre in France, four months earlier. Putten is a small municipality, some 11km (7 miles) north east of Amersfoort. A resistance group of unclear origin attacked a German staff car containing Wehrmacht officers during the night, for reasons which never became clear. One officer and one resistance fighter were killed. As ordered by Luftwaffe General Friedrich Christiansen, Putten was enclosed by German troops on the next day and most of the population was raided. Women were kept in the church while over 670 men were held in a nearby school and an egg depot. At first, there was no plan of what to do with them.

The men were transported to a concentration camp in Amersfoort later that day. Here, fifty-eight men were released for reasons of health. Humanity was not the reason. Medical care meant additional cost which the Germans tried to avoid systematically. Meanwhile at Putten, over 100 private houses were set on fire by Germans and Dutch SS. Next, six men and a woman were shot. The other women were released from the church in the evening. It was decided in the next few days that the men – who had had nothing to do with the attack – were to be transported to Neuengamme camp near Hamburg. On 11 October, 601 were put on freight trains. In transit, thirteen jumped off and managed to return home. None of them was ever tried or even charged.

From Neuengamme, 588 were separated to almost ten other nearby camps, as if in a German camp like Neuengamme there was insufficient room. There was always room in any German camp and, if needed, a new camp was erected. The inmates were given inadequate, filthy food, poor shelter, insufficient medicine. Some worked in nearby factories, other in water regulation jobs at the Elbe River. Of those from Putten, 540 perished and of those forty-eight who returned alive in 1945, five more died shortly after. For this war-crime, Christiansen was sentenced to twelve years in the

Arnhem court of military justice in 1948, of which he served only six, for health reasons.

It was a sweet revenge when Hanns Rauter himself was wounded seriously, in a mistaken assault by the Dutch Resistance in early March 1945, close to Arnhem. Two of those involved in the attack were defected Austrians. They operated in their uniforms to mislead Rauter's guards while their Austrian language was Rauter's. The aim of the Dutch was to seize a Wehrmacht truck, but in the dark they were just too late to find out that they had stopped a staff car, while Rauter was too late to find out that he was trapped. As a retaliation the Germans shot 278 Dutch prisoners. This was fully in line with Rauter's existing orders in the case of such a surprise attack.

Of these, 117 were shot the next day on the site of the assault. The other 161 were killed in several jails and prisons in the next few days. The victims were picked from their cells where they were held in captivity just for such special purposes – to be killed as a revenge, on very short notice without red tape. Many a victim was not told why he or she was to be shot. Rauter was taken to hospital and left behind by his countrymen when the Netherlands was liberated. He had not recovered and was taken prisoner. He was tried, condemned to the death penalty and shot in 1949, under martial law because the civil death penalty was abolished in the Netherlands in 1870 and has never been reinstated.

Both murderous events are another comparison with Heydrich in the sense that after he was assassinated in 1942, all 340 village people of Lidice near Prague were killed on Hitler's order. The small village was completely erased and a number of surviving children, orphans now, were sent to SS families living in Poland.

The price to be paid for peace without effort was a tough one.

Chapter Nine

Scarcity

Caroline Kuiper took an active part in the daily life of her family. Certainly this added to her self-confidence when outside school although she didn't encounter war conditions every day. Her father was employed at ENKA of Arnhem, which produced nylon. It is Akzo-Nobel today. Caroline retains a good picture of daily life in Arnhem as the war progressed, which can also be seen in documents in the NIOD institute of Amsterdam. She clearly remembers that life in general and the way people related to each other hardened. Gentle manners disappeared as the war progressed, certainly as long as there was little hope of liberation. People grew tougher, ruder sometimes, less tolerant certainly. The behaviour of train passengers exemplifies this as well as emphasizing shortages at the same time.

Some electric trains had separate doors over which hung small 'In' and 'Out' signs to help efficient entrance and exit of the carriages. After war had broken out, passengers continued to obey such signs. But as petrol, rubber tyres and parts were hard to obtain or unavailable to non-Germans, the number of private cars on the roads dwindled rapidly and more people had to travel by train. As a result, more people needed seats and this led to packed trains and standing room for many. At times, people were unable to board the train at all. Boarding any train often became a kind of wrestling match of shoving and pushing, unheard of before. It was no different in the plentiful city and suburban trams. The 'In' and 'Out' signs disappeared from the trains and did not return after the war.

Typically Nazi enforcements and curtailments appeared in the slipstream of the Heinkel bombers of Rotterdam – it was as if they were aware in the back of their minds that Hitler's Thousand Year Empire was to be short-lived. Even on the day of the Dutch surrender, and while Dutch (and French) troops were still fighting Germans in Zeeland province, German banknotes were declared legal tender in the Netherlands. They were not replacing Dutch money, but enabled Germans to pay for anything in their own currency, privately or as an occupying force, using the *Reichsmark* (RM). One and a half RM equalled one Dutch Guilder. Even before *Reichscommissioner* Seyss-Inquart took office on 25 May, a few curtailing steps had been announced. They were among the first steps of the Nazi boots.

A wide variety of important steps in the financial sector followed as well, paralyzing international trade while assuring the traffic of Dutch valuables to Germany. They were announced about once a week over the next few months. Politically, the entire legal system was blocked in early June, 'in order to prevent any damage to the interests of the Kingdom of the Netherlands'. Was this the best way to avoid Dutch lawsuits against the German state involving the Netherlands or the Dutch people? It certainly was. Shortly after, certain sections of German criminal law were also applied in the Netherlands.

The Germans were the only authority in the country, but only by force and were not considered the new government. As soon as 'the occupiers' had settled ('the occupier' or *'de bezetter'* is what the Germans of 1940 to 1945 were referred to then and now), they needed Dutch construction workers to improve or expand existing airfields, aviation and air force facilities; and to build new ones, too. Next, they ordered blockhouses at the North Sea coast as part of the *Atlantikwall*. Dutch building constructors welcomed these contracts from the navy. The Germans also ordered men to work in the coal mines in the Maastricht area. The last trace of unemployment problems from the 1930s all but disappeared overnight.

That, of course was welcome, but caused controversy as well. Was the German occupation good after the slump of the thirties, or was it bad? Should the Dutch cooperate with the Germans, or ignore them. Cooperation was considered collaboration and a few who considered political cooperation, under pretext of trying to make the best of it, silently turned away in most cases, in one occasion on order of the Germans. Only later, the Germans recruited and rounded up men of eighteen and over to work in Germany; and children, as will be seen.

Large-scale rationing of various products, which had been available without any restrictions before the war, became standard practice under the

German occupation and affected every single citizen. Shoes were the first to be rationed, even in mid-May, only a week after the Dutch capitulation. A few of these rationings remained in force until a few years after the war, as a result of total disruption of production, sales and exports of products like these, during the war – which was exclusively due to 'the occupier'. There had been no shortages at all in the Netherlands since substantial flooding from natural causes in 1916, which in fact became the starting point of the large polder winning process in the IJssel Lake after 1918. So, the German rationing of all kinds of products as soon as they occupied the Netherlands resulted from their impounding of supplies and distortion of economic life in the Netherlands. These steps were also made effective within days of

City trams became the main transport all over Europe during the war, as the number of privately owned cars and buses dwindled. In Arnhem, city trams of all lines came together at Willem's Square at 15-minute intervals, enabling quick transfers in every other direction. This tram Number 2 is headed for a steep district with several offices, where quite a few people already owned cars when the war broke out.

the German occupation. They were clear signs of the Nazi boots on Dutch ground.

All private and business telephone and telegraph services were cut off within the country and to the outside world within days of the invasion. Long-distance calls were not automated then or until many years after the war, while many people were not connected to the public telephone network. Long-distance calls were put through by local operators. This could take several hours. There were a few exceptions, though; telephone calls with Germany and other countries on behalf of German communication remained in force. A regular telephone network was also maintained between the power plants in the country. With a few 'illegal' extensions, this network was also used, in the course of time, by the Resistance. This enabled the Resistance to pass on intelligence to London. It was more important that for Resistance purposes long-distance calls were hard to detect. Such calls were at local rate which revealed one local call only. Certain public emergency calls continued to be in service as well.

In Arnhem, as Caroline recalls, all primary necessities of life came 'under pressure' as war progressed. All kinds of commodities became scarce, rationed or not available at all. By this, she means daily food and food variety, milk, tea and coffee and other drinks, clothing, furniture, coal, housing. Virtually every single kind of food was rationed. Coal gave way to peat, or worse, during the last winter of the war. Coffee was replaced by a mix of grain and chicory and it had a bad taste. Rationing and food availability is about average for what the Dutch people as a whole were experiencing, but in contrast to the Netherlands and most, or even all other occupied countries, there was no rationing in Germany until late 1944. German coffee however was a surrogate and kind of stinking, 'not to be boozed' as the Dutch say, until the sixties.

Housing quickly became hard to find, as much as elsewhere. This was not immediately as a result of large-scale destruction by warfare yet, but since very many construction workers and those in parallel jobs, such as painters, plumbers, were needed elsewhere. Newly built housing in a new Arnhem suburb south of the Rhine was first offered to those from Rotterdam who had lost their homes in the German bombing raid. Many blocks were finished just before the German invasion of 1940 and hardly any new ones were built afterwards. In 1939, there were 2.2 million private houses or apartments in the Netherlands for a population of 8.9 million in January 1940. About 80,000 were vacant for several reasons and purposes. One such reason, as usual everywhere, is to ensure there is an emergency reserve.

During the war and until the liberation, 86,000 houses or apartments were destroyed and another 42,000 were seriously damaged. The Hague was the worst affected, losing a total of 7,662. This was largely because of demolition as ordered by 'the occupier' and also to construct defences which would give the Allies a hard time in the case of an invasion, something which the Germans feared throughout the war. Another cause resulted from a serious bomb attack made in error by the RAF in March 1945 and yet more were due to failed launches of V-1s and V-2s. Amsterdam and Arnhem were placed second and third respectively regarding loss of living accommodation. The main cause in Amsterdam was the deportation of tens of thousands of Jewish citizens who never came back because they were murdered, as well as resistance workers. In Arnhem, it was warfare, first during Market Garden, then in April 1945 when the city still had to be taken, while the Canadian forces expected great German resistance.

Because of all houses destroyed until 1945, a quarter of all Dutch families no longer lived independently. They had to find shelter, or lived apart in the same house with other families in one way or another. This living apart in the same house was called 'living in'. No one was very happy to admit that they were themselves, or had others, living in. In fact, this was the most serious and longest scarcity of the twentieth century in this country.

As a rule, rationing in the Netherlands was enforced when supply decreased to 80 per cent of the average, which usually was taken to be pre-war demand. In this way, every citizen could acquire what he needed, not just the highest bidders, even though less was available. A few items such as sugar and dried peas and beans were rationed in 1939, as a precaution, but that was all, and even that was abandoned in 1940. During the war, rationing of all food, fruit, all kinds of fuel, clothing, furniture, construction materials and much more for individual needs was introduced, always assuming that these items were available.

Certain products like bananas were not rationed as they were not imported any longer. So, getting a banana after the war for the first time was a surprising experience. Rationing itself then became the responsibility of the mayor and local civil servants. Being occupied meant that the country was virtually cut off from all imports of food and raw materials from overseas, colonies and other countries alike. In the early occupation, even off-coast fishing on the North Sea was prohibited by 'the occupier'.

Sales of petrol and tyres for cars and bikes, leather products, woodworking, tar and tar products, narcotics, coal gas and coal gas generators were prohibited in the country from mid-May 1940. The first rationing of shoes followed five days later, liquid fuels the day after. The Dutch population was involved again when in mid-June textiles were rationed, bread, flour and paraffin oil on the next day. Rationing was a problem since many people did not understand how the system worked and how many coupons were to be submitted for certain quantities of bread. Bakers had to explain this to almost every single customer and what was the customer's share in this. Life became even more difficult when rations were reduced in exchange for the same number of coupons, as certainly was the case with commodities like bread, milk and meat as the war progressed.

Bread remained rationed until a few years after the war. Even in 1946, when my father had to sort out the coupons for different items he sold, he had to stick the coupons on large sheets of special paper. In exchange for these sheets with coupons, he could obtain the different kinds of raw materials needed. It was a difficult and time-consuming system. Also, no shopkeeper who supplied goods in exchange for rationing coupons (and payment, of course) was in a position to expand his volume of trade, unless he was able to add new items. The only small profit was that at home. Until Market Garden there was bread most of the time. My father did not allow us more or better bread than other families could get. The first time I saw pure white bread with its exceptionally delicious taste was several months after the liberation.

In the next month, rationing also became effective for leather shoes, all kinds of groceries, butter, margarine, soap, meat, sliced cold meat, Dutch cheese (there was no other), certain baked products, earthenware, glass objects and electric articles such as irons. But this was not the end. In January 1941, even matches were rationed while in the next months, milk, potatoes, jam, mashed potatoes and cocoa were added. Several more products followed, such as tobacco products in May 1942. Fish became the latest to be added, in July 1944.

These products were not rationed in the Netherlands because of German impounding alone, to convince the German population that the nation had become an *autarky* (fully self-supporting) as Hitler had announced. It resulted also from their warfare and losses of general supplies during Allied bombing raids, as well as to compensate for lack of work force. Thousands were taken into the armed forces; hundreds of them were lost every day. These measures affected Dutch traders and producers as well. When, for whatever reason, earthenware was rationed, it immediately decreased production of a family member's artistically-minded pottery which was already affected by lower sales and exports.

The more members in a family, the more rationing sheets were available, albeit less in the case of young children. Obviously, small children could apply for less than older children or their parents. Each sheet consisted of a large number of small coupons. It was indicated for what kind of products they were intended (even sweets!) and they were marked and numbered, as the sheets were securities. Generally, each week, in each town, it was announced in meticulous detail how much food and other commodities were available in exchange for payment and how many coupons were needed. In turn, shopkeepers including butchers, bakers, milkmen etcetera, had to organize these small coupons and glue each of them, in order to qualify for new supplies, commodities and raw materials. There were strange exceptions however. Small boys were allowed only one to four eggs during 1942.

Caroline remembers:

'Each week the newspaper was spread on our table to spell out what was available in the city during the next week. Relevant coupons were cut out, as it was frequently announced which coupons were valid in one particular week. They could be redeemed in that particular week only. Any extras were not available. Our daily pattern of consumption was much in line with the rationing, while in a large family like ours, careful planning was a must. Sometimes supplies turned out better than expected. More often it was disappointing. Supplies shrank as the war progressed.

'There were separate coupons for a wide variety of products, for households and industries'.

Caroline and her brothers remember only too well how small piles of slices of bread were pinched for each member of the family, twice a day.

'The younger you were, the smaller number of slices. And woe betide you if you tried to sneak one slice from a wrong pile. You were criticised without mercy by all others at the table, simply because there was not really enough for everyone! When hot meals were cooked at home, food was partitioned by our mother at every single plate, also according to age'.

Since life had to go on as normally as possible, many families in the cities managed to rent a piece of ground to be used as a vegetable garden, outside town. Caroline's father owned one across the IJssel River, some 7 kilometres (just over 4 miles) from his home. I visited this garden one afternoon and it surprised me how much variety there was in what my uncle grew on behalf of his family. And of course, as well as increasing variety in their diet, they were free from rationing as well. One problem was always how to prevent vegetables being stolen from such gardens, as there were only outside fences to protect them.

The next challenge might be how to prevent any harvested vegetables being collected by special, official checkers who preferred to 'believe' that such fruits and vegetables were intended to be sold on the black market, another expression of the scarcity of everything. Anyone too shy or frightened or otherwise unable to fight their corner were always at risk of having their vegetables or fruits impounded without a fair reason, simply because they were taken by surprise.

Jackie Muusse, the girl who lived next door to us, was my best friend, at less than a month younger than me. Only some thirty-five years later she and her two elder sisters discovered we were second cousins as well, as one them told me. Some surprise, thirty-five years later! She was nearby when the dog was shot and she was as shocked as everyone else. During the war, Jackie and I played together very often, in the back yard or at home most of the time, or in the street, sometimes joined by one or both of her sisters. Their mother, aunt Mary as I called her, often prepared cocoa for us in the morning. This was an exceptional delicacy. It looks like the nuts were still imported. But it was ground cocoa mixed with sugar. And there was more. On birthdays of the Dutch royals, five and later six times in a year, Jackie and her two elder sisters got big orange bows in their hair. But because of the risks, the three girls were strictly forbidden to go in the street!

Jackie told me:

'We also played aeroplanes in our back yards. Running around with our arms spread. A few boys joined us so we flew in formation. My mother observed it and she did not like it'.

A nice trick of resistance by aunt Mary was to show her little girls how to collect the seeds from the orange marigold flowers in their back yard. Then, when the wind blew from the south, she told her daughters to throw and blow handfuls of marigold seeds to their neighbours on the north side. No trouble with the first neighbours, who were loyal Dutchmen as well. But much joy in the case of those next door, who were Germans. Today, Jackie tells me that she was not even aware that those people were Germans. They were just referred to as 'not to be trusted'.

Jackie's father grew kale and a few more vegetables in his back yard. They were happy. But, as her mother said, unfortunately he could not 'grow' the smoked sausage most Dutch love to eat with kale. It is a prize winning specialty among Arnhem's butchers. My father did not have a vegetable garden. Being a family of two grown-ups and a small boy only, there was less need for growing extra vegetables, I expect. Besides, since he got up very early every working day, he used to take some rest in the afternoon. This left little time for minding vegetables. In the autumn of 1943, he managed to lay his hands on a rabbit. He made a hutch for the soft beast. The rabbit was taken care of well. One day my father took him somewhere and I did not see the rabbit again. But the next Saturday, which happened to be Christmas 1943, the taste of 'the meat' was special and delicious. Rather than growing vegetables, my father was a spicy home cook as well.

In summer, daddy pedalled to other, somewhat more distant family-members, who lived in the Betuwe and grew different kinds of fruit for a living, like apples, pears, cherries, and plums. The Betuwe is one large garden for fruits, vegetables and potatoes. It is also the cradle of America's well-known coleslaw, which is a mixture of apple, cabbage and dressing. On a few occasions my father took me with him on his bike, to his family-members to buy some quality fruit.

Cycling had become uncomfortable and dangerous, as tyres were scarce and rationed since May 1940. Dangerous, rattling tyres made from wood replaced them when the old ones were worn out, with people who could afford this clumsy luxury. Others, which were many, rode the bare wheels which is very uncomfortable and risky. From Arnhem, pedalling the Betuwe to cover some 30km (19 miles), he constantly looked up and around if planes were overhead. If so, cover had to be found right away. This must have been the bright spring or summer of 1944. Once at his destination, he paid a so-called family price, if anything at all, and we returned home with a good deal of fruit.

I loved to join him, also as the family hid a black 1930-style automobile. They lived in a beautiful and very old farmhouse that is still kept in good order and also had a few orchards around the little village church. I was involved in doing some sort of 'work' in the orchard which I enjoyed, as it kept me busy. A few boys, somewhat older than me, lived there too. The black car was hidden from impoundment by pressed bales of hay against the farmhouse. But when I was there, some bales were put aside, so that I could be a passionate driver in that old square automobile. I loved it and it must have left behind some memories. Half a century later, in the mid-nineties, we visited this farm again, still owned by those distant relatives. A descendant showed me around and he remembered 'this little boy from Arnhem' who was such an avid driver of his grandfather's hidden automobile.

Tobacco was rationed from mid-May 1942 and was ended for women early April 1943. Tobacco coupons were no longer supplied for women and they could no longer buy cigarettes legally – on behalf of their husbands and sons. Many women in this Calvinistic part of Dutch society were not supposed to smoke in those days, so it was rather a strange step. But by 1944, tobacco was no longer available to anyone. So if possible, men planted tobacco in their yards at home, as did my father. Planting these in a vegetable garden away from home was a risk, because smoking was standard behaviour for almost all men. This self-grown tobacco often was not really fit for cigarettes, as it was not fermented and cut properly. Non-smoking women turned to smokers again during the days of liberation, when Allied soldiers supplied cigarettes and chocolate freely; and got many young ladies in return, many of whom were far from modest, or Calvinistic.

A German order was that production of food in any year had to be sufficient until the harvests of next year. However, much that was needed had always been imported from other European countries as these items were not grown locally in sufficient quantities, or sometimes not at all. Tomatoes for instance were hardly grown in the Netherlands before 1940, but traditional domestic fruits were grown widely. So, shortages arose quickly. German replacements were not to be expected, of course. This resulted in the cultivation of several additional agricultural products, though this was often not all that easy under wartime conditions.

Land for commercial agriculture however was a smaller problem, since the new and future large polders in the IJssel Lake were destined exactly for that purpose. One had been newly finished in 1940. A second polder was finished in 1942. Half of these two rested against the old land, the other half in the case of the first polder was protected by a long dike. This was the Wieringermeer Polder in North-Holland, between the towns of Den Helder and nearby Medemblik.

Like in other areas of the Netherlands, growing several kinds of new products became very successful in the new polder. The small polder-town of Wieringerwerf expanded to 118 per cent of its 1940 numbers of farm houses because of this. All produce could favour Dutch customers. Then came 17 April 1945. Germans blew up the dike under the pretext of an imminent Allied invasion. Such a threat was pure nonsense at any stage of the war. It took as long as 48 hours to flood the entire polder and 309km^2 (80sq.miles) of land was lost. Everything that grew was spoiled within two days and virtually every house, farm, store, church and other public building was destroyed.

Wieringen was a new, small place in 1940. But 118 per cent destruction as compared to its size of 1940 was unique. Even in Germany, no city suffered

Men (and one woman) queuing outside a shop in The Hague in a typical wartime scene. This was Nieuwstraat, where coffee beans were roasted (*koffiebranderij*) and tobacco was cut (*tabakskerverij*). The queue is most likely for tobacco, since coffee roasting was no longer allowed after 21 February 1941. Availability of every commodity was very poor, so when shops like these suddenly had stock, customers arrived from all over the city. Chances are that tea was no longer available when this picture was taken as all three were typical colonial products.

over a 100 per cent destruction of all structures as compared to 1939. People throughout the Netherlands were really shocked by this large, new token of villainous brutality, including those in other areas which were hit by German inundations themselves.

Meanwhile, there were also some kind of replacements, surrogates as they were called, for a variety of standard or household requirements. Bread, of course, was the most important commodity. Next to flour, bakers also had to process certain quantities of different raw materials, in order to supply sufficient loaves of bread in accordance with demand – and legislation. Until the war, wheat and rye bread were the foremost types, like in all European countries. Rye bread was less popular. Since much wheat was imported, supplies were curtailed dramatically after 10 May 1940.

Something new was so-called government bread. It was of specially ground wheat mixed with potato flour and ground legume. Being used to light brown wheat bread, people disliked government bread because of its dark colour, sour taste and doughy touch. But there was little to no choice. Late in the war sawdust was added and personally, I experienced bread of even worse composition after Market Garden. That, of course, was late in the Famine Winter of early 1945. And when, by way of a joke, I asked a baker for a government bread many decades after the war, the man was close to being insulted and almost showed me the door.

Another surrogate was clay and a layer of sand, to replace soap. Pumice from the Indies was also used, but not everyone felt fit to treat himself with pumice. Zinc was used for coins from 1941, to be finally replaced by nickel in 1948. Cardboard replaced leather for shoes and even coffins, as wood was impounded by 'the occupier'. Twisted paper was used as a replacement for rope. After the war in the Arnhem area, boys found twined pieces of real rope which originated from the parachutes of Market Garden. Most of us had never seen such beautiful rope and asked, 'What is this?' In contrast, sometimes an older person in the Netherlands who buys some light natural rope today, will still check if it is made from hemp or paper, although certain shops present their merchandise in paper bags with paper rope.

Meat was scarce as well, since most stock was impounded by the Germans. Cattle stock had decreased by 88 to 84 per cent in 1944 as compared to 1939, hogs to as little as 32 per cent of 1939, poultry to 10 per cent. Consequently, production of milk, margarine, cheese, meat products and eggs decreased dramatically. In turn, the cost of living rose (from 100 Gilders in June 1939) to 170 in June 1944 for foods, 260 for (paper) shoes, 280 for clothing, to 1,000 for beef. These are the price-levels until Market Garden. Later, horses, sheep and other small animals were slaughtered as well which was not done previously. Cats were sold as rabbits. No precise figures are available of living horses of which thousands went to Germany. Initially, horses were used to pull Dutch cars, for lack of petrol. Later, the Wehrmacht used them to pull their trucks and artillery both within Germany and near the fronts, to compensate for their own lack of fuel. These shortages resulted from Allied bomb raids and were effective in slowing down German land traffic.

Coming to Caroline once again, she recalls that her mother sometimes told her and a brother to go to some place in the city of Arnhem when a special sale was announced.

'Mum herself would come later, carrying the required rationing coupons and the money. Such a special sale usually meant a sudden extra supply of food or goods which were in great demand generally, such as textile for making clothes, but the nature of the announcements could mean anything. Rumours like these spread through the city with the speed of sound, and in a wink there were long queues in front of shop doors on the day announced, as in many cases the commodities had not arrived yet. And yes, there we stood just like that, as 8 or 9 year olds between many older grown-ups. Which all tried to push us aside, these little children, to buy commodities before supplies were sold out.

'So when after an hour or so our mother arrived, we first had to tell her in a clear voice which persons in the queue had pushed us aside. And this, of course, caused people to object and swear at us, telling our mother that I was lying. But then my brothers or girl-friends with me, and sometimes some other people as well, were there to tell who was really telling a lie. This was a relief to me, since I often hardly had the guts to say, even in a normal voice, that it was not me who told a lie.'

Arnhem was no exception to general practice during the war. In fact, this kind of behaviour was not any different from what happened at the railway stations. Besides, many Dutch are aware that queueing the Dutch way is a far cry from the more civilised practice at the other side of the North Sea.

A somewhat peculiar form of scarcity, an attempt at psychological control in the first place, was the German order of 1940 to replace all London street names on the popular Monopoly board by Dutch street names.

Chapter Ten

Frontlines in the Skies

The major confrontations were on the high seas, with those in the air following behind. But they side-lined Dutch citizens in the sense that they were entirely unable to influence these air fights in one way or another. As a result, there were the beams of search-lights at night which caused fear. There was bombing, dogfighting, and ack-ack from guns all over the Netherlands for the duration of the war. This resulted in an average of three Allied or German aircraft destroyed every 24 hours, a total of about 5,500 aircraft, including planes hit over Germany which did not make it back to their British bases or even the North Sea. This compares with Belgium, where about 4,000 aircraft crashed. Today, aircraft wreckage and bombs are still recovered from Dutch soil or water. Surviving relatives are notified then and at last know what happened to their loved ones.

Although there was no invasion by British forces on a Dutch beach until November 1944 at Walcheren Island, the RAF push-back of the Luftwaffe in 1940 prefigured the kind of counter-attack that certain Germans must have expected. So, the Luftwaffe had started to construct, expand and revitalize Dutch airports and military bases as soon as they were able to in the spring of 1940. In fact, no less than 22 airfields were in military use during the war of which four stood out.

Deelen is just north of Arnhem. Enlarged by the Germans to a *Fliegerhorst* it became the largest Luftwaffe base of night fighters and bombers in the Netherlands. The reason was the route the Allied bombers followed when they entered Dutch air space for bombing raids in Germany, mainly when aiming at the industrial Ruhr area. German fighters based at Deelen attacked Allied bombers in the area from Arnhem to Nijmegen. Deelen was also where the Luftwaffe had installed one of its westernmost and most important radar stations. There was another one in Arnhem, close to the road bridge and less visible from the air.

Rather special is Gilze-Ryen air base, between Tilburg and Breda in the south. Following intensive espionage from the air and on the ground, the Luftwaffe decided to expand Gilze's facilities to become one major air base for bombing raids on the UK, once the Netherlands was occupied. It became one of the largest in Europe in 1940, where almost every type of German plane was based. Luftwaffe fighters based here attacked Allied planes from UK bases head-on, almost every day and night during the war when they crossed the Dutch 'enemy coast ahead' in the southwest delta.

RAF bomber missions to Germany and to strategic targets in occupied countries, including the Netherlands, increased significantly after Air Marshal Arthur T. Harris was appointed Commander in Chief of RAF Bomber Command in February 1942. Most RAF bomber missions took place at night. In the same year, the USAAF 8th Air Force joined in, albeit very hesitantly in the beginning, but operating in daylight as they preferred. Consequently, familiar but terrifying noises were in the air over us almost continuously, both as heavy Allied bombers, smaller tactical bombers and fighters went out – mostly in formation – and when they returned. But there were individual warplanes as well, either on separate missions out and back, or in dribs and drabs as damaged planes limped home, sometimes on fire.

It is true that much fighting took place in the Dutch skies as well as on Dutch soil, years later. The country itself also was subjected to many bombing raids. After those of the Luftwaffe in 1940 and again in 1944, some 600 raids were carried out over the Netherlands by the Allies. Most targets were industrial; harbours and railroad junctions and in most cases there were few or even no civilian casualties. In thirty-nine raids however there were at least thirty-eight civilian victims and many airmen died as well. The bombs did not always reach their targets, or did not explode at all – the so-called duds. Unexploded bombs from the Second World War are still found today. Planes and flying fuselage also fell everywhere, causing damage to houses and people. Statistically, almost three aircraft per square mile, including over water had crashed by the end of the war.

In Britain today the bombing raids on Germany are often seen as unnecessarily cruel acts of war. To most Dutch people, this is different, particularly to those with war time memories of their own. While suffering from the boots of terror, to the Dutch, the Allied raids over Germany meant

Small monument at Aalten, East Netherlands, commemorating five RAF airmen from a Stirling BK767 who crashed there on 26/27 June 1943. The inscription on the monument reads *Vliegen voor de vrede*, Flying for Peace.. Those killed were F/O. B.H. Church (21), Flt.Sgt. W. Th. Davis (21), Flt.Sgt. F. Mills (20), Flt.Sgt. W.H. Thompson (21), F/O. J.F. Tritton (28). Two crew members who had bailed out over Germany were taken prisoner: F/O. K.A. Nielson and Flt.Sgt. E.G. Taylor. During the war a wreath was placed on the sight with the message, *Gebroken vleugels, onsterfelijke roem*, 'Broken wings, immortal glory'. The crash was one of thirty-nine over the Netherlands on this particular night. The bomber was from 214 Squadron, based at Chedburgh, Suffolk.

that every hit was a small step closer to the end of the war. In Dronten, a city in Flevoland province, on a tract entirely reclaimed from the IJssel Lake, where in the sixties, many wrecks of ships, Allied planes and even a 1927 Ford were found, there is a small monument in respectful honour of the Allied airmen who lost their lives while flying over the Netherlands. According to British sources, this is the only monument of its kind on the continent but this is not entirely correct. In the Netherlands, there are more monuments for Allied and some Dutch airmen, in most cases commemorating the loss of individual aircraft and crews. One of these is near the Oosterbeek war cemetery on behalf of Canadian airmen lost in action on 17 September 1944, although no names are listed.

A war was on and as soon as there was an air alarm with screaming sirens, children like me were instructed to run home from wherever they were playing in the street or the back yard. Air alarms had been in place in the country since 1933, and were used every hour of every day and night from 1940 to 1945, when needed. They were abolished after the liberation and restored during the confrontations of East and West; the Cold War. They are tested at noon on the first Monday of each month and their sound is much different today. But the wartime air alarms have made a fearful impact on many people, never to be forgotten. Among them, Jackie Muusse's eldest sister, five years older and 80 years old at time of writing, tells me that she still shivers with fear, every noon on the first Monday of the month. She certainly is not the only one.

Gerrit Lourens, aged between 7 and 12 years during the war, lived at Renkum, a small town to the west of Arnhem and recalls:

'If RAF bombers flew about our country at night, they made a very heavy, monotonous buzzing, almost like a grumble. And a raid in which Emmerich was targeted, could be watched from the top of our house'.

Emmerich, a Dutch town which until 1814 was called Emmerik, is the last German town downstream on the border of the Rhine. The small town was settled over 1300 years ago. It contained a chemical plant which the RAF targeted on 7 October 1944. It is said that 91 per cent of the town was wiped out in the attack, making small Emmerich one of the most decimated of German cities. Emmerich was also bombed in 1943, as Gerrit remembers. At Renkum, he was some 38km (24 miles) away in a straight line northwest across a flat river-land and says:

'The red glow and the flames in the distance are etched in my memory. Ashes and burnt wisps of paper came floating as far as our area'.

But in May 1940, winds carried the other way, to the northeast. From Rotterdam as far as Utrecht.

'We also saw the beams of the searchlights from Emmerich, as well as of Deelen air base close to Renkum, and the flashes of the ack–ack explosions from both. We also noticed when planes were hit and burst into flames'.

The Rhine and its branches such as Waal and IJssel are always dangerous to swim in, because of many eddies.

'So we were forbidden to swim in the Rhine every time after bomb raids in Germany. The water could be brown and filthy and sometimes even corpses of human beings, human limbs or animals floated by. The buzzing sound of those aircraft as well as the V-1s from later in the war, is still with me. A few years ago, during a commemoration of 17 September 1944, several big aircraft formations passed our skies and when this happened, the deep fear I felt during the war came over me again'.

Today, though Gerrit is 82, his memories appear just as clear as they were when he told of his experiences seven years ago. Someone else, a second cousin, feels just the same when talking about the air alarm. Bad, fearful memories of World War II never fade away. So many decades later, people only have some difficulty in remembering dates or years, but certainly not the events themselves. Next to sounds, people also seem to remember particular tastes of the war.

Janny Bakker lived in Eindhoven not far from Philips' electronics manufacturing plants. Between Janny's house in those days and the plants there was a railway embankment. 'Those plants were RAF targets more than once', she recalls. The complex concerned was where radio tubes were manufactured, ordered by the Germans. In fact, it produced one-third of the German requirements during the war. Consequently, Philips was a major strategic target until 1944. This made living in the area very risky. But just as in Britain in the early stages of the war, and in Germany during most of the war, few people moved to places believed safer. An exception is the Germans in the Ruhr area, of whom many moved to Middle Germany, (the GDR after 1948), and Silesia, beyond reach of the Allied bombers for much of the war.

Janny was 8 years old at the time. She recalls:

'During raids we rushed to the bathroom with a kitchen pan on our heads. I don't think this was useful protection against falling rubble, but it protected us from pieces of whitewash coming from the ceiling during explosions. At night, when planes flew over, I was often very scared. Especially by their heavy buzzing, even though I knew that they were headed for Germany. For fear, I sometimes trembled so much that my parents allowed me to join them and huddle in bed between them. Meanwhile my younger brother did not worry at all and slept without interruption.

'One evening, we were forced to leave our house for fear of becoming a target. Maybe we were alerted by the police, I do not remember. Together with many others we took shelter in a dry ditch, my parents lying on top of us to protect us. Bullets flew all around and many fearfully started to pray loudly. Yes, Maria of course, we were in the [Roman Catholic] south, weren't we? On 6 December 1942, a boy was killed in one of the heaviest RAF bombing raids of Eindhoven, in our area. Just the evening before, on Sinterklaas' Evening, this boy had acted as a Black Piet, and had come to our house as well'.

During this raid, 148 citizens lost their lives.

Bomber formations of several hundreds of Allied planes regularly attacked Germany. The capabilities of these bomber formations and their bombs cannot be compared with those of these days. Over Germany, there were so-called millennium, or thousand bomber raids, targeting one single destination such as Cologne, Hamburg or Berlin and causing unimaginable sorrow and damage. There were also raids in which about 1,000 bombers, or more, flew together until they had reached German air space and then separated, heading for different targets.

Several cities or other targets were regularly attacked. Berlin was bombed 464 times and in 1942 also suffered a few Soviet Air Force attacks. The RAF and USAAF bombers never flew a straight path to their targets. They zigzagged to confuse and surprise the Germans in a very wide area until the very last moments before attack. Thus, there were many false air alarms in communities, scaring as many Germans throughout the country as possible, which was another strategy. When a few days later news came that a certain city had been targeted, many Dutch chuckled. No peace without effort, also in Germany, albeit enforced by others than Germans. The Germans did not react the same way when a Dutch city was bombed. Like a stern uncle, Germans would seize every opportunity to point out how much damage their 'so-called friends' had done.

Flak-turm (anti-aircraft gun tower) in Berlin showing the German's heavy, and very effective, 88mm gun, as well as a number of shells and its operating crew. Two white rings on the barrel indicate that it had shot down two aircraft. The photograph was most likely taken for propaganda purposes. In Germany, most men employed in such Flak-batteries were students, about 16 years of age. Note their oversized coats, which were not made for soldiers of their age, and their different trousers. Their young age was another example of Germany's 'Total War' once the eventual outcome became clear: there would soon be Russians in Berlin instead of Germans in London and Moscow.

Large formations of aircraft took several hours to pass overhead. Their low speeds, 300km (180 miles) to 500km (300 miles) per hour caused this, as did their many different base locations. So, while the foremost bombers in a big wave of attack were over Germany or nearing their targets, such as the industrial Ruhr area, the very last bombers in line still might be about to take off, or to rendezvous. Bombers from different bases in Britain often flew in a close and extremely long formation over the Netherlands, more so in bad weather and limited visibility.

Of course, such lengthy and rather slow operations seemed to us to permanently fill the skies, both at night, when the RAF and RCAF were outbound, and in the daytime when USAAF forces took their turn. The share of the Canadian crews is often underplayed, while the RCAF played very important roles in the Battle of Britain, anti-submarine warfare on the Atlantic and many bombing raids against German industries. Using British-built aircraft mainly, the only outward differences were the RCAF roundels and they were hard to distinguish from the ground. The Canadian army were credited for their 1944–45 share in liberating the Netherlands and bringing food. It was the fourth largest air force in the world in 1944, having a significant share in bombing Germany and attacking German forces.

It wasn't just a steady stream of aircraft, four droning radial engines per plane – it was a very heavy and terrifying droning and it took many hours. The entire spectacle was even more terrifying for people on the ground when anti-aircraft guns and German fighter planes got involved. As the war in the air increased, which was certainly true when Air Marshal Harris was in charge of Bomber Command in February 1942, Allied fighters escorted the bombers and added to the very fearful noises and violence to destroy Germany's industries and cities. There were also separate fighter and tactical bomber missions for strafing in North France, Belgium and the Netherlands.

Harris ordered area bombing to German cities, also called carpet bombing, thereby copying the Luftwaffe bombing on Guernica in 1937. An eye for an eye. But unlike the Dutch, who, in 1940, certainly did not want the risk of more cities to be bombed and people killed, the Germans never gave in, thus leaving them with cities destroyed up to 100 per cent in 1945, north to south and west to east, of which Emmerich was a clear example.

Next to escorting, there were separate fighter, tactical bomber and bombing missions of targets in North France, Belgium and the Netherlands. But since the Germans responded to virtually all Allied approaches until late 1944, there were also sudden onslaughts of Allied fighters, counter-attacking German fighters, searchlights, ack-ack-guns and planes coming down. This yelling and whining and the heavy explosions of the grenades depended on where you were of course. Arnhem, Nijmegen, Eindhoven and the areas around may have suffered the most of all cities in the Netherlands. Meanwhile, the bombing raids on Germany were a relief to the Dutch, not to be deplored. '*Daar gaan ze weer*', it was often said, 'There they go once again,' well aware that such missions were sacrifices rather than holiday trips.

Air Marshal Arthur T. Harris, head of RAF Bomber Command, 1942–1945.

Meanwhile, what goes up, must come down as the British scientist Isaac Newton concluded, to which it may be added in this context that what takes off, must return to base. Most of those hundreds of planes returned to base several hours later after the crews had completed their missions. Many aircraft and their crews, however, did not. They paid the price of an attack. Their return flights from missions over north and middle Germany often took into morning sunlight. By then, many bombers had been damaged and dispersed by Luftwaffe fighters and anti-aircraft guns over Germany.

The Allied crews and planes could still be attacked again as they returned over the Netherlands. This was particularly harsh as their crew-members were cold and tired after the perils of long flights, when they had dead and wounded on board or had witnessed fellow crews bailing out or breaking up in mid-air and crashing. The bombing raids cost the lives of innumerable crews and their planes. In all, well over 160,000 Allied airmen perished over Europe, including those whose planes had been hit, crashed into the North Sea and were never recovered. 'Lost in action'.

The entire spectacle of the streams of planes was even more terrifying for people on the ground when frightening anti-aircraft guns and screaming German fighter planes got involved. Small wonder that young children in the countries involved often had to leave their beds at night – 'Mum, I cannot sleep!' Sleep was broken either because they had woken and were afraid and could not get back to sleep, because of the uninterrupted heavy droning, the explosions and the dangers involved, or when awaked by their parents and others to be dragged quickly to some kind of shelter, perhaps a basement, if heavy gun fire, air fights and bombings were nearby. Children like me asked their parents what the bombers were heading for all the time. My father's answers were guesses, of course. Essen, Hanover and Berlin are the names I remember hearing most. He couldn't care less which city it really was.

In many cases, the nearest shelters were in people's homes, under the stairs or in basements. But this was not really safe. Fragments of planes and pieces of grenades could hit or penetrate through roofs, windows and walls with very loud, heart-rending bangs. Next to parts of planes, there could be crashing bombers, their bombs or fighter planes as well. It did not happen every day or night, but chances were always there. People had to be careful and they were afraid all the time, especially if they lived in the areas where this particular and exceptional kind of warfare was common on an almost daily basis. Even so, not every Dutch citizen was afraid of British or US war planes. Many photos were taken from RAF cockpits of Dutch citizens in broad daylight, on roof tops or in open fields, waving at the pilots. Of course these Dutch citizens had to be careful not to be spotted by Germans or collaborators, and run the risk of being locked up and tortured on charges of conspiring with 'the enemy'. It was not the enemy, but an ally which might cause a lot of damage.

Clearly, children were not allowed to go very far from home or out of sight. They had to come home right away when air raid alarms were heard, or seek shelter wherever possible. But children had to go to school, which left them vulnerable virtually all through the day. Nor was it much of a surprise that anyone could go for a long walk, into a park or to the woods. There was always a danger of sudden air activity which would force them to take shelter somewhere. We were living in fear most of the time, while those born between 1937 and 1945, did not know what a quiet life was, until after the war.

Caroline Kuiper can remember more than I do, because she was ten in 1944. Her brother John was eight and between them, they can recall a lot of detail:

'Once the shooting in the air started, there were no safe places. And as the war progressed, shootings and explosions increased in force.

Which included the frequency of warning signals, sirens, over the city. But when we heard the sirens, we might have heard the rumbling of bombers even before, day and night, like a distant thunderstorm.'

John remembers specifically:

'The scariest moments were those when the sound of their engines seemed to be interrupted. As soon as the engine sounds came again, which were shrieking screams, you could expect sound of impacts and explosions. They terrified us to death. The ground vibrated and window panes burst when the explosions were nearby. At the same time, these explosions caused personal relief, as our house was not hit.'

Caroline says:

'Very often we had to take shelter under the stairs in our house. It was the safest place, our parents believed. But when we were playing in our garden or in the street, we had to take cover behind small walls of people's front gardens, if available, or under shrubbery. In fact, our freedom of movement became restricted more and more. We could go out in daylight and play on the street as it was very normal in this years, but after eight in the evening we all had to be at home. There were increasingly more curfews, in the spring and summer of 1944 almost every day. We were allowed to leave our home for a few hours of the day only. It was just enough to do some shopping. At home, all doors and windows were kept locked. In most cases the heavy curtains were closed as well, to avoid pieces of glass from coming into our house when windows broke after a bomb exploded nearby. Those curtains prevented the glass from flying about.'

John, a retired Boeing 747 captain recalled:

'We had to be careful every time when we went in the street. An air raid alarm could be heard any moment, which caused many to run into the streets to find a place in a public shelter. Sometimes there were false alarms. But we also learned that bombs fell at random on houses, instead of what might have been the real targets. Then, inevitably, we learned about people killed and wounded.'

Certainly one week to remember is Big Week. It was the code name of a week-long Allied air operation against German targets that took place between 20 and 25 February 1944. USAAF 8th Bomber Command from Britain and 15th USAAF from Italy took part during the day, with the RAF taking over at night. They intended to wipe out as much aviation and some related industries in Germany and Austria as possible. The aim was to establish full air superiority by the time of the Allied invasion on the continent. Over 3,800 bombers from both forces were deployed with various targets. They were accompanied by hundreds of hard hitting fighters. The operation was aborted prematurely because of bad weather.

USAAF 8th Bomber Command was re-designated Eighth Air Force on 22 February 1944. Their commander was Major General James Doolittle, famous for the first Tokyo Raid in April 1942. The very first performance of what was to become 'The Mighty 8' had dreadful results, however. Second Division, which consisted of 177 big four-engine bombers, B-24 Liberators, was assigned to bomb aviation and related industries in Gotha and beyond in Central Germany. They were surprised by German fighters who attacked them over the North Sea, before the Dutch coastlines. This had not happened before. The B-24 bombers were well-armed, but were still in the process of forming. The last bombers were not even airborne while fast fighter planes such as the powerful P-38 Lightning fighters, agile P-41 Mustang fighters and tactical bombers and long-range heavy P-47 Thunderbolt fighters had not yet joined the bombers either. The Mustang was used by the RAF as well – it was initiated by the British Purchasing Commission.

Due to sudden bad weather and strong easterly winds over Germany (160km, or 100 miles an hour in the upper atmosphere), they were ordered to abort and return, just as they entered Dutch air space. But the leading flight officer missed the order due to continuing, malfunctioning radio communication. He carried on, as the weather in the Netherlands was quite clear with only light cloud. It took about half an hour before the leading flight officer was confirmed and convinced that such an order came from his own HQ, not from a German source. But by then the bombers were over 160km (100 miles) across the Dutch coast, over Germany in most cases, where the weather was very bad.

In the circumstances of an aborted raid, crews were allowed to find and bomb so-called targets of opportunity inside Germany. It was strictly forbidden to seek 'targets of opportunity' in the Netherlands (designated targets in the Netherlands or any other places in occupied Europe were not targets of opportunity). The crews were well aware of this. One of their targets of opportunity instead of Gotha, became the city of Münster, 66km (40 miles) into Germany and in a straight line from Enschede, its nearest Dutch town.

Two more such targets were the small, thirteenth-century towns of Goch and Cleves, each very close to the Dutch border, near Nijmegen. The bad weather conditions over Germany resulted in several of the bomber groups losing of track of each other and their own positions. But rather than returning straight to base, dropping their loads over the North Sea, as some of their comrades did, most of them tried to find German targets for their cluster bombs and incendiaries.

The result was that bombers first flew around in circles and then, instead of finding German targets, mistakenly bombed Enschede, Arnhem and Nijmegen. The first city to be bombed was Enschede, 73km (44 miles) northeast of Arnhem. While believing that they were over Münster, thirty-one out of thirty-five Liberators dropped twelve incendiaries each there. This resulted in almost 40,000 small bombs, without a warning or even an air raid for the city's population. A wide area of the industrial city caught fire. Forty people were killed, almost 150 wounded and 725 people were left homeless. The district was rebuilt after the war but, amazingly, the same district was blown up in May 2000 when a firework stock exploded. There were 23 killed, 900 wounded and 200 houses were destroyed.

The crews had failed to check if the cities were the German cities they had selected. And when they found out that they weren't, by looking down and comparing with their maps, it was too late in three cases. Deventer might have been a fourth unwanted target, but escaped this tragedy. It is 36km (21 miles) northeast of Arnhem at the IJssel River, 106km (66 miles) from Münster. At the very last moment the crews spotted that it was anything but Münster. Fortunately, those twenty bombers involved here were able to drop their bombs in a field just across the IJssel river, as pictures from one bomber reveal.

Caroline Kuiper had just had left her school in Arnhem, for lunch at home, when she heard the rumble of aircraft in the distance. Heavy planes came from the northeast. Given the time of the day, many citizens of Arnhem must have witnessed the next moments of the low flying bombers and their wide open bomb doors. Caroline was not in her usual small group, which included two of her younger brothers. The sudden rumble frightened her and seconds later there was the air raid alarm. 'The sound of the alarm came in waves, up and down. About the same moment, AA-guns started to fire', she says. Shortly after, she was scared to death because of a series of heavy explosions in the distance and many more nearby. This was at 1.24 in the afternoon.

Caroline's parents and little brothers were very anxious when the aircraft dropped their deadly loads. Where was she? Fortunately, it was not very close to Caroline's usual route between school and home. The nearest bombs fell about a kilometre, or little over a half mile away. Her father, who happened to be home from work, described the impacts as 'an infernal racket' in his diary. Caroline had rapidly taken shelter in some bushes in the freezing front garden of a house, hiding her face until the whole thing was over. She had to stay there, she knew, until a second air alarm, the 'all clear', was given. She did not wait that long. Caroline relates:

'I was shaking with fear, trembling all over, even more so because I was on my own. I turned to the street when the sound of the planes faded away and I raced home as fast as I was able to.'

And yes, her family at home were very relieved to see her!

My own mother had taken me, just four and a half years old, for a walk to a friend of hers on this cold and clear February morning, not thinking about any air activity for a change. There were sudden dangers all the time and we got used to it. We did not live like rabbits after all, jumping from one shelter to the next. The lady we visited lived in an apartment, a few kilometres from our home. It was not all that far from where Caroline walked home.

After some time there was this frightening air raid alarm. My goodness! And this time, it was different. There was much more of the buzzing sound of many heavy planes than usual. It was much closer. Next, and completely unexpectedly, there were very heavy explosions, fairly nearby and rapidly coming even nearer. There was no time to decide what to do.

This time, as it appeared later, the crews believed they were targeting the German city of Goch, 38km (26 miles) away in a straight line. But they were wrong. Goch is to the southeast of Arnhem. Goch does not border a major river as Arnhem does and as the crews clearly could see, both from the air as their pictures show, and on their maps. Goch did not at all look like Arnhem. Still, fifty bombs from twelve *Liberators* fell on Arnhem – in a residential area south of the Rhine; into the Rhine itself, sinking two long barges and damaging a third; in another district nearby; at a marshalling yard; in a rubber processing plant and on the city's coal-gas works. All within a few kilometres. The tanks at the gas works exploded, making flashes and even louder noises, even though these works were not hit seriously.

We were only at about 350m (1140ft) in a straight line from the nearest houses hit. There were tremendous explosions, the house shook, windows rattled, there was panic and screaming within seconds among the three (or more?) in the apartment we visited. Screaming from fear, I raced from one corner to another until my mother could grab my arm, pull me under a table, and then drag me under a flight of stairs. I managed to wrench away and started racing around again, looking out of the windows in the front and the rear of the apartment. This was as dangerous as hell, of course. Looking in the distance one moment, I saw a plane falling straight down. My cousin John saw a similar crash in the same direction, but it is hard to say if we saw the same plane. Fighters were shot down more often, either by ack-ack guns or by other planes.

One window pane shattered and fragments of glass flew around. My mother managed to get hold of me again and pull me under the stairs. 'Take it easy, relax,' she tried her best to calm me amidst the heavy explosions and then, 'Just try to imagine it is a thundery shower.' An unforgettable phrase! Was I supposed to not know the difference between a thundery shower and bombers after about four years of war – all my life? But she was just trying to calm me down and what more could she do, as a desperate parent?

A USAAF B-24 Liberator dropping its deadly load.

A few of those thundering bombs exploded so closely that we expected the next one to be on our roof or next door. It could so easily have been. The ordeal seemed to have no end, but then it was over – just as abruptly as it had started. It was a very surprising moment, this sudden empty silence. We all wondered what might be next, without hearing anything. This exceptional moment of silence in which there was no next explosion still fills me with a mixed feeling of overwhelming fear and a small piece of hope. But the intense buzzing of the bombers quickly faded away, like taking to their heels after a nasty trick. For years I have believed that the raid took an endless half hour. It only actually lasted a few minutes, I later discovered. Carefully, we walked to the window at the rear of the apartment. For a few moments it was very, very silent outside, even though among us there still was a lot of panic and tension.

Then, people started to come out of their houses to look around. Municipal fire engines and ambulances could soon be heard, as well as

German vehicles. All around, there was desperation, turmoil, confusion, even at such a distance from the real disaster, a few hundred metres. People wanted to get an impression of damage in the street, but damage was limited to a few broken windows and ripped off roof tiles. Some other people were still panicking and ran about. Somewhere closer to the area hit, someone ran into the street without having pulled up his trousers, we understood, as he had been on the toilet when the bombers hit.

In the two small districts struck on both sides of the Rhine in Arnhem, fifty-seven people were killed instantly. This included all members of one family as cousin John recalls – something that happened too often in countries that were bombed.

'One victim in this particular family was a classmate. Like us, he was at home for lunch. Some time later we took a look at the ruins, still smouldering. We were appalled at what we saw. Two other families lost some members each.'

Many dozens were wounded. In all, 463 people lost their homes. The damage of the gas-coal works deprived the inhabitants of Arnhem and a few surrounding communities of coal-gas instantly.

This lasted for several months, as parts for repair were hard to get or not available at all. Instead, the city of Arnhem supplied electric cookers to those families did not have one of their own. But electric cooking instead of coal-gas requires quite some adjustment, says Caroline.

'It is faster and it caused much irritation, quite a few times in the beginning, because of potatoes, milk and so on getting burnt.'

It was the kind of bombing which the Germans lived with for years, and on a much larger scale, with the obvious difference that Germany had caused the war and had provoked retaliation.

A few minutes after Arnhem, Nijmegen was also hit. Twelve Liberator bombers struck viciously at the heart of the city. Streets were busy as it was lunch-time, and there was little time for many to find shelter. Unlike today, shops were closed for lunch and could not offer shelter or protection. The

Allied bombs were far more devastating than the German bombs of 1940. Bombs fell at random in a large area in the city's centre and on the railway station, destroying a wide area. There were several fires, wiping out a large part of the city's centre. There were hundreds of victims within just a few minutes. The results in Nijmegen were devastating. Many of those in the streets had tried to find shelter in basements, but they were hit and killed as they ran, or were buried under collapsing structures. Much of the tower of the city's old church collapsed.

It was like Nijmegen had been hit by an earthquake. The number of direct fatalities in Nijmegen is estimated at 766. Many died of their injuries later, so the total rose to an estimated 900. There were several hundred casualties though accurate figures were never available, like in Arnhem. They included people from other towns and a few Germans. They excluded some people, who had simply disappeared from the face of the earth. Missing for good. Among the dead there were over 100 little children who were hit in their school. A large part of the old city centre was completely in ruins. This was far worse than in Arnhem or Enschede, although the raid in Nijmegen lasted a few minutes as well. Nijmegen is believed to have suffered the second largest number of casualties in a bombing raid in the Netherlands, after Rotterdam in 1940.

The city was not prepared for a disaster of this size. Nijmegen needed much assistance by emergency services from several other towns. Not only were more fire fighters needed, so were ambulances, medical supplies and many hundreds of coffins. They were forwarded from everywhere. Hospitals in Arnhem sent five surgeons and some nurses on secondment to Nijmegen to take care of the wounded. The dead were buried a few days later when identified, taking up several existing graveyards a few days later. The Germans and Dutch national-socialists however tried to take advantage of this bombing raid. Some members made a vulgar show of their presence in the city. The Germans had posters printed in which the message was: '*Van je vrienden moet je 't hebben!*', or: 'Count on your *friends*!'

At the same time, Germans suggested that the bomb raid was executed with approval of the Dutch cabinet in London. In fact, they knew nothing about it and were not even aware that German cities had escaped this onslaught. The Germans were the very last to produce posters like that and make phantasy remarks. Their propaganda and their opinions had little impact, as ever. In fact, when American and British troops entered the city almost seven months later, they were cheered like nothing heard before.

The bomb raids on the three cities were reported to the Dutch government in London the next day. There was a serious protest, although it had to be careful under the circumstances. The protests went as far up as Roosevelt and so they should; it was a very serious matter. Dutch indignation in London was great, especially as it was not the first time (or the last time!) when Allied bombers hit wrong targets. Little is known about the aftermath of these three major errors, both in diplomatic and USAAF circles, in spite of several studies by different investigators, even in recent years.

The first raid in error, which unintentionally took the lives of many Dutch citizens took place in 1941. On the night of 4 October, between 106 and 130 people were killed in Rotterdam by an RAF bombing of the harbour area. Some twenty-four victims were never found, probably due to available

'Count on your friends!' German poster after the three very negligent USAAF bombings on 22 February 1944.

identification techniques in those days. Another large number of victims fell in Rotterdam, when on 31 March 1943 about 400 people were killed in another careless USAAF bomb raid near the harbours. This one took place shortly after the so-called Norden bomb sights were applied, to improve bombing security. The system was not as good as it was believed by air force authorities and was removed by the 8th USAAF before the end of the war.

Two weeks later, on 16 April 1943, eighty-five people were killed in a RAF bombing of Haarlem. While railway workshops were the real targets, a nearby district was hit. In North Amsterdam, 185 citizens were killed on 17 July 1943 in a USAAF bombing – the real target was the nearby Fokker aircraft plant. Almost two months later, 11 September 1943, a suburb of Breskens, a harbour city in Zeeland-Flanders, was hit by RAF bombers and 199 people were killed. There were many more such bombings in error or at least bombings which caused many collateral victims and damage. As will be seen, there also was a Luftwaffe bombing of the city of Eindhoven in September 1944, causing the deaths of 227 civilians.

The third worst in the country in numbers of victims, albeit one of the last, was an RAF bombing of The Hague on 3 March 1945. Incorrect coordinates, the information for the targets of the bombs, were given to the crews. The real targets were V-1 and V-2 launching sites in a wooded park in The Hague – in which the royal palace of Huis ten Bosch is the only complex. Due to the error, a nearby suburb was bombed. At least 520 people were killed and 344 wounded. Around 20,000 were left homeless after 3,250 residences were burned out, many other houses were damaged and could not be lived in again.

Many people died or lost their homes as this was a big residential area, where most houses and apartments were roomy. Many families had given shelter to people from elsewhere in The Hague, where houses had been torn down to build defences against an Allied invasion. Dutch defence specialists point out that such an invasion would devastate most of the country because of the salt sea water and thus, would benefit nobody. Bombs also hit many places way beyond the area. A new American Embassy was built on one such bomb site in the 1960s.

Bombing raids on the Netherlands killed approximately 6,150 men and women of all ages. Luftwaffe raids may have cost the lives of about 1,350 people, while Allied bomb raids were around 4,800. There certainly were not bombing raids in the Netherlands every day, but there were attacks in one way or another almost every day. In retrospect and unlike several pre-war cabinets, Queen Wilhelmina is known to have been a strong advocate of good armed forces. But what did pre-war politicians both in London and the Netherlands, and military leaders who were put aside, think, in retrospect, when bombs again fell on the Dutch people? There is no peace without earlier effort, is there?

Chapter Eleven

1944 – Summer of Hope

It took just one quarter of the year – in fact it took just the summer of 1944 from D-day on 6 June until just after 17 September. During that summer, it was hoped that the war would end soon. There had been a lot of activity in the air since Big Week in the second half of February, aimed at establishing air superiority. It was a clear sign that the Allies were preparing for an invasion on the continent, whenever and wherever it might be. The general aim of the Allies was to gain air superiority and to paralyze the entire railway system, by damaging as many locomotives as possible. In turn, the Germans executed large-scale floodings in the low western part of the Netherlands, starting in early May, as a 'precaution' as they said, to resist an Allied invasion. The first weeks after D-day constituted hope for millions of Germans as well. But, strange as it may seem, not a hope of being freed from the Nazi dictatorship and the war which it had caused.

But something unusual happened in our house on 6 June. In the bright light of the afternoon sun, my father suddenly jumped from his chair while shouting with joy. 'The Americans have landed, the Americans have landed', he cried loudly, with unusual enthusiasm, hands and arms raised in the shape of a V. He must have been listening to the radio. In my view those '*Americans*' were something exceptional. Had I ever heard of *Americans* before? Had I ever seen my father be so enthusiastic before? It is very unlikely in both cases, for fear that I, a four year old boy, might be a risk for my parents. What kind of ears might hear this? Also, it was just not my father's nature to be very outspoken. Besides, soldiers of other nationalities had also landed in Normandy. Was he mixing things up in his excitement?

Yet my father was quick to tell this time why he was so excited that *the Allies* have landed as he said later, when he explained what all this meant. All that he told me was exceptional, as I found out decades later, when interviewing relatives. Jackie Muusse from next door, twenty-eight days younger than me says:

> 'I am sure I remember our parents heard about the invasion and maybe they had dropped a few words about it. But what this really meant, I do not remember. They did not say very much about it, I think. There were so many unfamiliar words during the war and we were small children.'

Caroline Kuiper about her family: 'No, we do not have any memories'. Two of her younger brothers agree with Caroline. But Pauline, still another Kuiper niece who lived at Velp, remembers the news very well, she says:

> 'Our father took his radio from its usual hiding place, to listen to the BBC's News Hour programme, and he was so astonished when he heard the exceptional news of the landing.'

Her father was my dad's brother. She had a younger sister, who lives in Canada now. 'They have landed', her father told his wife and their two daughters. The meaning of this was very clear to all. An Allied landing had been the talk of the town throughout the country, for the past year at least. Janny Bakker also remembers hearing the news.

> 'I was ill in bed. My parents had placed the bed by the window. The lady from next door knocked at our window and said, "They have landed". Just that and we all understood her message. It caused great stir in our family. A very happy atmosphere came over our house instantly. The end looked in sight.'

The BBC's broadcast was heard throughout the Netherlands and everyone was talking about it. Most Dutch had heard the broadcast despite the German ban on owning a radio or listening to one. 'They have landed!' everyone whispered to everyone else, as though spreading so-called 'unwanted' news might lead to an arrest as well. Many were sure that 'it will be over soon now'. No explanation was needed, no one asked 'What do you mean by that?'

This was Operation Overlord. Many Allied soldiers were lost as they never made it much further than the beaches. But what they left behind was freedom. No Dutch army soldiers were on the coast on 6 June 1944. Dutch navy elements had off-shore duties in which almost forty merchant and navy ships, including torpedo boats, were involved, as well as Netherlands Naval Aviation Service aircraft. Dutch losses were relatively high. Twenty-five men were killed, eight B-25 Mitchell bombers were lost. Two gunboats, known as *Terrible Twins*, fired in support of Allied troops on the beaches. Off the coast one old 1926 cruiser was sunk to serve as a breakwater.

Over 1,700 Dutch men and women had escaped to the UK since 1940 – from the country, from offshore ships and overseas places. It was not a big number as compared to about 30,000 French, 18,000 Danish, 6,000 Belgians. The escaped Dutch joined some various forces such as the RAF or the Navy in exile. Prince Bernhard, Crown Princess Juliana's husband, became a pilot. About 1,200 men initially, the Princess Irene Brigade, trained at Wolverhampton, landed in Normandy in August 1944. This Dutch brigade and a Belgian one liberated the small Normandy town of Pont-Audemer on 26 August. Then, in late September, came the very worst part of the German occupation. They ordered eviction of all citizens from Arnhem and some western towns after Market Garden and brought more scarcity, more terror and starvation like never before in the history of this country.

In a long series of Allied operations, the German power position in Normandy collapsed. Goebbels got the answer when, by 8 August, Le Mans was taken by the American First Army. General Omar Bradley said: 'This is an opportunity that comes to a commander not more than once in a century. We're about to destroy an entire hostile army and go all the way from here to the German border.'

It indeed marked the turning point in Western Europe. According to Eisenhower in his book *Crusade in Europe* written in 1948, the Germans lost 200,000 men, killed, wounded and missing and another 200,000 as prisoners between D-day and reaching Paris, in the Battle for Normandy. Around 1,300 tanks, 2,000 pieces of artillery, 20,000 non-armoured vehicles as well as over 3,500 aircraft were destroyed. One German army commander, three Corps commanders and fifteen divisional commanders were killed or taken into captivity. These numbers were subject to change and according to later sources, an estimated 514,000 Germans were killed, missing, wounded or taken prisoners. About 15,000 armoured vehicles and related equipment were lost, including almost 900 tanks. Not one but two German armies were defeated. Hitler then ordered withdrawal from Normandy. In late August, all four Allied armies were on the Seine river and took Paris on 25 August. For the Germans, the tide had turned against them definitely and they knew it. Many Dutch had hoped for a much earlier break-through. Peace, however, does not come without effort as the figures clearly show. The generation of Allied soldiers of 1944 had fought its way and had defeated Nazi-Germany.

It would have been about this time that my father started construction of an air-raid shelter in our back yard. He may have been inspired by the heavy fighting in Normandy, while he could well imagine what might be ahead, in view of the air activities over the past years over Arnhem. There was much more of it since the early spring of 1944, as the Allies – obviously unknown to us on the ground – prepared for air superiority over the Luftwaffe when the day of the big Allied counter attack came closer. D-Day, in short, a

German column destroyed near St. Ormel, Normandy, by 1st Polish Armoured Division, July 1944. A battered German tank is on the left, a Sherman on the right. Clearly visible is the use of horses by the Germans even at this stage of the war. The Allies, meanwhile, were no longer using horses.

military term of which the meaning has puzzled many old and young Dutch for years after. It was not until later that I discovered that the 'D' stood for Deliverance.

My father's idea was a modestly sized air-raid shelter to reduce both vulnerability and time to construct with available, affordable means. It was stuck half way into the ground, to give somewhat more protection and with sandbags for additional strength to the sides and the top. It was big enough for the three of our family and a few more, such as our neighbours and their three daughters. Or my own grandparents, who lived several kilometres from us in the very heart of Arnhem. At least one neighbour may have been involved, to help my father in the construction, although neither my neighbour Jackie nor myself remember anyone in particular.

But once he or both of them started digging, others came along, asking what happening, which resulted in one compassionate smile after another, because who would believe the Allies would to come to Arnhem first!! Oh no, most home-grown generals reasoned that after Paris, they will be heading for Berlin straight away. My father must have disliked those remarks, as he was somewhat touchy about that kind of criticism, but having seen war himself very nearby in 1940, he continued to work.

When finished some short time later, this shelter with entrances on both sides – like a real tunnel, so as to make allowance for a blast, was a most attractive addition to our garden. Jackie and I plunged into it, out and around, as she remembers as well, playing hide–and–seek. This was it! Being small, we could stand right up inside. And we could sit on the bales of straw which my dad had arranged for comfort. We did not play there often because soon this shelter was needed for real – and left behind for good. My father however, could take pride in having completed this useful home-made idea for his family in time.

According to one BBC radio report, an Allied vanguard was said to have reached the city of Breda in the Netherlands on 4 September. This of course would mean that the liberation of the Netherlands had begun. Many Dutch citizens are known to have taken their national red-white-blue colours, the traditional orange streamers and other pieces of decoration, from hidden places, in order to hold out as soon as the first Allies came in sight. There are photographs of people clogging a street – the Dutch variant of queueing! –

in front of a shop where flags were sold. A few telephone calls were made, but in Breda no one confirmed the arrival of any Allies. But rumours spread quickly. Someone had 'heard' that Allied paratroopers had landed near Rotterdam, even The Hague. Others copied this so-called news, happy that they were able to share something very, very pleasant. But there were no paratroopers near Rotterdam or The Hague, not since 1940.

More importantly, while the city of Antwerp and the harbour were taken, the harbour could not be entered and remained useless for Allied supplies. The mouth of the Scheldt river, which flows from Belgium into the Dutch Wester-Scheldt, was in German hands and remained so. Ghent was taken on 5 September. But there, Allied advances west of Antwerp came to a standstill. Supplies were growing short. The men were tired after their long and rapid advance from Normandy and, last but not least, their top officers focussed on crossing the Rhine now, their next step. Strangely enough, they did not intend to liberate (Dutch) Zeeland-Flanders as well, the southern bank of the Wester-Scheldt.

This enabled a large part of the German 15th Army to escape across the Wester-Scheldt and settle on the north banks, the islands of Walcheren (Vlissingen) and South-Beveland. The estuary, a tidal river, was saturated by Dutch, British and German sea-mines, some even from 1914, and could not be cleared. So, and contrary to Eisenhower's belief, the entry from the North Sea to Antwerp remained in German control. Sea-mines are still reported in the Wester-Scheldt every week, even today.

Many other disordered and dispersed German military reached Arnhem from all points of the compass, on their way to Germany. They came by train, by truck, on horses, with horse-carts, on stolen bicycles, on foot heading back to 'Jerrica' as Germany was called by many in Dutch ('*Mofrika*'), a contraction of '*mof*' which is an age-old Dutch term of abuse for Germans, and (backward) Africa: *Mofrika*. Today, the word *mofrika* is known by few and is no longer used to denote our decent neighbours. In 1944, they were all welcome to go there!

Besides, *Reichskommissar* Arthur Seyss-Inquart ordered all German civilians in the Netherlands to move to the east of the country from 4 September, to enable them to get away to Germany if needed. He himself moved to Apeldoorn, 26km (15 miles) north of Arnhem. Anton Mussert, leader of the Dutch national-socialists, copied Seyss-Inquart's order for his own disciples.

The Dutch who lined the streets in almost every town saw them leave and were elated. Dutch collaborators and Germans mixed and mingled with hundreds of thousands of other German military personnel who, individually in most cases, also hurried to their *Heimat*, a very important thing for a Nazi, meaning 'home' but so much more than we can convey in English. Many of those Germans however, fell into a trap at Arnhem, if not earlier. Most had escaped from Normandy, Paris, northern France and Belgium, either from frontlines and naval bases, as well as personnel to fire V-1s at the French and Belgian coasts, or as occupying forces in those countries.

Rather than considered deserters, vulnerable to being fired upon, or fugitives, they were efficiently assembled, re-organized and sent to barracks and other places in a wide area north and northeast of Arnhem, to be available when needed. As well as Wehrmacht, they included many Luftwaffe ground and air personnel who were 'on foot' as most German planes had been destroyed, from the air or on the ground. They were unforeseen reinforcements, unnoticed or seemingly overlooked by Allied Intelligence. They joined the regular German forces which had retreated from Normandy. In Arnhem however they were quickly sent in a different direction, to prevent demoralization of troops arriving from Germany or the Dutch western parts.

The same day, 5 September, became what some Dutch still call *Dolle Dinsdag*, Mad Tuesday, although there was more of it on the previous Monday. Even though not a single Allied unit had yet reached Dutch soil, Germans and their Dutch accomplices, both men and women and from all over the Netherlands, grabbed their private possessions, burned the files of their atrocities by the thousand, cleared out the houses they had stolen so proudly in 1940, left the offices, quickly stole another Dutch bike or carrier tricycle and rushed away to Germany, head over wheels. The closer to the German border, the longer the streams of men and women in their much-hated Wehrmacht green, blue or black uniforms, or plain clothes, with 'poor consciences' – criminals of all kinds of varieties, to be blunt. Meanwhile, people threw rocks at the windows of these abandoned private houses, offices and – in the case of collaborators – their shops, or broke into them if they could.

On Mad Tuesday however, they were even more annoyed as locals lined the streets of Arnhem and many other cities. Most citizens were happy to see them go after four years of something no-one ever wanted to experience again. Many called these sudden refugees thieves, traitors, nasty skunks, filthy bastards, 'nasty prostitutes' and what have you, when circumstances allowed. They were called names because of their own invariable habit to snarl at people in loud voices – like many still do without restriction today – and because of having drafted 'soldiers' fourteen years of age and little older, as we had seen marching in our streets. Nine out of ten women who had relations with German soldiers during the war were not prostitutes, by the way, but had genuine relationships. But politically their choice was wrong and many were weighed down under it for decades.

Collaborators and single women were laden with mockery and scorn. The worst kind of curses were shouted against these sudden 'refugees'. Some were even spat at by policemen, many of whom had been subjected to German orders, more than others, very directly for more than four years. But however violent, it was nothing compared to what other Germans and even more their female collaborators were dealt out in France.

The euphoria among the Dutch was short-lived. There were no Allies in the Netherlands. Only a few days later, most Germans and Dutch Nazi-collaborators started to return without having even reached German soil. But many, particularly Dutch collaborators, stayed in the east and northeast of the country. Filled with more hate of the Dutch and more hungry for revenge than before, they acted accordingly in the months to come. A fortnight later, on 17 September one German who took shelter among a few Dutch in Arnhem during an air-raid said, *'Jetzt kommt der Tommie. Das habt ihr Hollaender doch immer gewuenscht? Ganz Arnheim geht kaputt'*. ('Here are the Tommies. This is what you Dutchmen always wanted, isn't it? All Arnhem will be destroyed!')

Gestapo chief Hanns Rauter reacted to the joy of the Dutch by proclaiming martial law. This seems rather ridiculous as martial law, certain German laws and countrywide occupation had been in force in the Netherlands since May 1940. His 'martial law' was nothing short of even more terror. Gatherings in

A 'Liberation' party on Mad Tuesday, 5 September 1944. A circle of people dance joyfully in Rotterdam following radio reports from London that Allied forces had entered the Netherlands.

the street by five or more people were forbidden. Being in the streets beyond curfew hours (evenings and nights) was a fatal offence. If curtains were not properly drawn at night, patrolling Germans used to knock on doors with the butts of their guns and shouted: '*Licht aus!!*' ('Lights out!'). In the south of the Netherlands, men were rounded up to build reinforcements on behalf of the Wehrmacht. In Nijmegen it was announced that families – parents and their children – were to be locked up in concentration camps unless the heads of families joined the forces in support of the German military.

Something entirely new happened in Wassenaar, only 11km (6.5 miles) from The Hague, on the evening of 8 September 1944. Germans fired the first V-2 ballistic rockets in anger, aimed at London and Paris. The distance to London in a straight line is the greatest, at 510km (315 miles). Both cities were within range of the V-2 when fired from Wassenaar. Preparations for the first missile to be fired had started on 6 September. The rocket was launched from a trailer in a street lined with trees which made them hard to be traced, then, from the air. The RAF was well aware of the German developments of this '*Vergeltungswaffe-2*' or Revenge Weapon-2 and had bombed the test site in northern Germany, near Peenemuende at the Baltic coast, in August 1943. Development was then continued elsewhere in Germany, where they were found and bombed as well. The great promotor was Wernher von Braun, who was a member of the SS.

The first rockets caused a great stir on impact. They were fired to an altitude of 82–93km (51–58 miles). Speed on impact was three times the speed of sound. No one heard them, very few saw them and their rate of material destruction was high. It was essential that the V-2s should be eliminated.

Late in August, resistance workers in Arnhem were ordered from London to blow up all railways in the Arnhem area, but in such a way that they could be repaired at short notice. What a strange order; blow up tracks and repair on short notice. Nonetheless, they acted as ordered. All four railways to Arnhem including a half viaduct were blown away in the next few days. The Germans were furious and announced that if the perpetrators did not report themselves voluntarily by noon of Sunday, 17 September ten men would be picked from the streets and shot publicly. They were unaware that another surprise was being cooked in Allied kitchens, almost ready to be served.

Chapter Twelve

A Sunny September Sunday

It started as a quiet and bright day with autumn just showing its colours; Sunday, 17 September. It might be the last chance to enjoy the season, although we were well aware that a war as on and warfare was coming nearer. Yet, my father suggested a relaxed walk around our district. It was a risk really, since the partial blowing up of the railway viaduct in the week before. This was the day that the Germans had threatened that ten male Arnhemers would be taken from the streets and shot if the Resistance did not own up to their recent sabotage.

There had been a lot of air activity in the previous few days, but it was nice and quiet now. Mum stayed at home. Many went to church that Sunday. My parents had decided not to attend the service as the church was a long way away and getting to it was an inherent risk. Other relatives of ours, though, took those risks, including Jackie Muusse's family and Caroline's. In most cases, those attending were mothers, aunts and their children only. Husbands and other male family members preferred to stay in the safety of their homes.

We walked to the attractive and nearby park on the Angerenstein estate. During the war, the main building was the provincial headquarters of *Reichskommissioner* Arthur Seyss-Inquart, whose national HQ was in The Hague. Then, at about 10am, there was a short air alarm – the well-known and frightening, up and down yawning noise. Over the last few months it had signalled about every day the Allied advances coming closer, after the break-out in Normandy, the conquests of Paris, Brussels and Antwerp. My father took me back home rapidly. But at first, nothing special happened in the skies. Some short time after, the 'all clear'-signal was given – a long constant high pitch tone for over a minute at least. Was it a false alarm?

Then there was a second air alarm, less than an hour later. This one has become the last one in Arnhem's war time history. No 'all clear' was ever given. When we got home, we felt rather safe. No need to find shelter in our backyard yet. Mum heated up some milk for what was supposed to be my parents' coffee. Maybe there was milk or cocoa for me. Coffee wasn't my cup of tea anyway. But then suddenly, oppressively overhead we could hear very heavy plane noise. Aircraft seemed to be flying at rooftop level and we could hear sudden bursts of engines roaring. There were heavy explosions that came nearer and nearer. There was one at a nearby barracks, maybe a few actually. Then there was a sudden flash and then, very close by, BANG!

The air pressure this created made us fall to the floor. The house was shaking. A few windows shattered and just as back in February, I was frightened out of my wits. A bomb raid again? I didn't have time to think about it. One parent grabbed me and dragged me to the air-raid shelter in the backyard. There was no bright sunlight when we got outside. All I could see when I looked up was an unforgettable intense grey – the air was full of dust all the way to the shelter. It was flabbergasting. I was pushed into the dark inside, told to sit down on the straw and bend over. My parents covered me with their bodies to give me more protection. The heavy explosions continued outside but the sound was deadened. Being excited, all three of us were short of breath. A few other people also climbed into our shelter. A sunny Sunday had turned into an ordeal all at once and continued to become a disaster by the end of the same week.

The next real target was Seyss-Inquart's provincial office in Angerenstein park as previously mentioned. The office was hit even before we had reached our own shelter. It was set alight, but the structure has survived the war. Meanwhile, the heavy noises of planes and bombs were all around. It went on for hours. Roaring planes, shooting and frequent explosions. What was going on today? It all caused great tension among the few people in our dark shelter. Hell on earth is what it was. The war on our doorstep. There was much debating about what this was all about, but no-one knew or could work out the real reason. There is no recollection of how much time all of us spent in the shelter.

Then, my mother rose to leave. 'What are you doing?!', my father cried. 'I haven't turned down the saucepan of milk!', she replied. 'The milk?! Are you out of your mind? Stay here!' my father said. But he wasn't thinking properly and his efforts to persuade her to forget the milk didn't work.

Actually it wasn't the mess of boiled milk all over her electric hot plate she was worried about, it was the fact that the saucepan might cause a fire in the house that motivated her. She returned shortly after and got a good telling off, even though my father was happy to see her back. There was no chance of a fire, she said, as there was a power cut, at least in our house.

Actually, the power cut affected the whole city. Trams stopped wherever they happened to be and they never started up again. Virtually all tram cars were destroyed in the next months. The network was broken up after the war and trams were replaced by British-made trolleybuses four years later. Mum, panting with exhaustion, also reported that she had seen some broken windows in our and in our next door neighbours' house.

A few minutes later, some more people also pushed themselves into my father's shelter (which obviously wasn't such a joke anymore, now that they were invited to enter as well), because explosions were continuing in our area. All spoke nervously and it still was dark inside. I didn't recognize all of them and I disliked their sudden presence a little bit, as the space became cramped. Some of the voices were unfamiliar. Among them, I found out many years later, there were two Jewish women whom I had never met, who had been sheltered by our neighbours. A couple of the intruders had what was called a squeeze cat ('*knijpkat*'), a small green instrument with a spring button on top. By pushing this button repeatedly with the thumb, there were brief flashes of light. It was enough to see that most intruders were known relatives and neighbours.

Jackie Muusse meanwhile was not among them. I wondered where she was. A few more entered our shelter, certainly more than its limited capacity allowed. It was more of a private hiding place. I was told to sit on the ground. I felt that as an insult as I sat between pairs of feet in the dark. I wondered why so many more people had been able to join us. Of course, just one bomb nearby was enough to sweep all of us from the face of the earth. But there was no such bomb, albeit the one that had made us speed to the shelter, had caused considerable damage to the house at the lower end of the street. A young girl lived in that house and she was celebrating her tenth birthday. Her birthday ended before noon, when she was killed.

It has never been clear why that particular house in our street was the target of a fighter-bomber. Over the next few days, and even after the war, we were told that it was a secret SD office. It was an incorrect assumption, as the garden and the house were privately owned. But there was the Gestapo office of Angerenstein, although not really nearby. Another target might have been an office of the ENKA nylon plant just at the opposite of the Velperweg. But it is more realistic to assume that the bomb had actually been targeting Rauter's large, privately inhabited mansion at the Velperweg, about a 100m (300ft) away. That particular target was out by a whole block of houses. It hit our block!

Arnhem certainly was not the only place in the country visited by streams of light bomber planes on 17 September. They aimed just as much at selected strategic targets in all other towns which were to be involved in the Market Garden operation. Only a few minutes earlier, roaring planes had caused great panic in front of Arnhem's railway station. Waiters had just started to place small tables and chairs outside because of the lovely weather, when a number of Mosquito-like aircraft roared by, seemingly at rooftop level. Frightened almost to death, the waiters didn't hang about before they swept the pieces of business furniture back into their bars, shut the doors and sought cover.

Just a moment later, at least one tactical bomber had reached one real target. It was not the railway station. The target was a 107-year-old striking barracks complex in the heart of the city, called Willems *kazerne* (barracks) after King Willem I. It was an SS building. They hit the complex right in the heart with a number of bombs and rockets. One explosion after another was followed by a tremendous fire and there was a large number of victims. Some 250 young SS 'machos', as my parents called them, were said to be killed instantly. The billowing smoke of the burning barracks was visible in most parts of the city. A neighbouring restaurant with a high level of German patronage and their local friends was seriously hit as well. An uncle of my mother, a painter of art and collector of pieces of antique furniture who, with his wife, lived just opposite the barracks, was taken by surprise when his windows were shattered and the entire ceiling in his living room came down as well.

Many of the next targets bombed were strange ones. A few fighters sped to the northeast, one of which caused the bang in our street. Other raced towards the Rhine bridge, but continued east or southeast after having dropped a few bombs in the city centre. They intended to hit anti-aircraft sites as it became clear later, but on this Sunday people wondered what the real points of impact had to do with war. Like the failures of Ede, where so many civilians were killed, among such targets was an old people's home in the heart of Arnhem, as well as the city's nearly new, at only seven years old, theatre, on opposite sides of the same street.

Also hit were a small church, a warehouse and a hospital just a little further on, all by the same batch of explosives. There was damage all over and there were casualties among the patients of the hospital and among people in apartments living in the area. One school building was saved among a few blocks of houses destroyed, the strange fate of war. Nobody was inside, as it was Sunday. Nor were any visitors in the theatre at this hour. The hospital appeared entirely ruined after the war.

Fred Brons, the architect of the theatre and still living in Arnhem, was shocked when he was notified of damage done to his creation. He rushed to the scene to take a closer look, later on the same day. His luck was bad. He was hit by pieces of rubble coming down suddenly and he was killed. It was unclear what kind of targets the tactical bombers were after with regards to the local warfare. The damage to the theatre was limited and it was repaired after the war. Nearby, an old church, the Walloon church as it is called, was entirely ruined. Only the four walls were left in 1945, some of them seared by fire and smoke. It was rebuilt, although a great many years later.

Nearby these sudden ruins, a shop was razed to the ground. Only the basement was left and over the years it filled halfway with water from pipes, rain and snow. But following the liberation, people in the district used to warn one another, particularly the youngsters, never to go into this basement which was partly covered by the floor on street level. It was said that a dead soldier's body was still to be found in the basement so, as young boys, we tried to have a look inside this dark basement, sometimes. But due to the filthy, always bad smelling water, no one had ever seen this presumed soldier and we wondered if it was just a story. But when in the late fifties the last parts of the destroyed block of houses was cleared, remnants of a German soldier were found in the water in the basement, so that was one story that was true all along.

It was said that military objects and interests were the Allied pilots' targets. But there was little of this nature in the heart of Arnhem, except for the barracks complex mentioned and one more near our house. There were only a few anti-aircraft emplacements in the city. In the early afternoon, more violence was still to come, so there was no reason for us to believe that it was all over! A number of shops with apartments in a main shopping street were hit. More structures were hit, such as a marshalling yard, the same as in February 1944, as well as the railway goods station just outside the city.

The church service going on near the centre of the city was broken up when the second air alarm was heard. The vicar ended the worship with an emphatic 'amen!' and suggested the congregation leave. All those present squeezed themselves out onto the street, where the thundering ordeal, aircraft and Flak, was all around. It frightened people and they sped home as fast as circumstances permitted. They ran through the streets and when another plane or explosion was heard, they tried to find some shelter. Since the attacks were not being executed by a formation of bombers, there were moments between explosions. The worshippers, ordinary civilians now, used these moments to resume their spurts, until the roaring engines of another Mosquito were heard.

Nervously and full of fear, Jackie and her friends had to walk and run a distance of 2.1km (1.25 miles) before they reached home. They were unable to follow the most straightforward route, as some streets were full of houses on fire. So they headed for the neighbouring main shopping street, where a number of shops had been hit by bombs. Today, she recalls:

> 'Although it was a warm day, I was surprised to see some people lying under blankets on the pavement – or sidewalk. It was such a strange sight to me, seeing people sleeping on the pavement in the middle of the day!'

Were these actually sleeping people, as an older person she was with told her? No – they were victims, of course.

Further down the main street, Jackie and her family found the arterial northeast Velperweg route was blocked where the street was crossed by an elevated railway – the tracks to Germany. Right under the viaduct they noticed a dud. What now? There was no other route to get beyond the railway and there were dangers all over. Should they run and escape beyond the risk? Or run the risk of an explosion while under the viaduct which would have wounded or killed them all instantly? 'After some hesitation, also because of the dangers above us, we decided to run on quickly,' Jackie recalls.

But then, there was still the long open road to Velp and beyond, another 1,200m (4,000ft) until her home.

'Our mother was so happy when we safely arrived at home ... window panes were broken all over a wide area around our houses. Roof tiles had slipped and there was sand and dust everywhere in our street. So, we must have been lucky not to have been hit by tiles or glass when speeding to your shelter in the back yard.'

Halifax bombers lined up to tow Horsa gliders at Tarrant Rushton, Dorset, 5 June 1944. Throughout the war, the RAF ordered over 4,200 gliders. The scene is similar to the preparation for Market Garden three months later, when Dakotas, as well as adapted Halifax and Stirling bombers, were used to transport and tow gliders.

Their next step was on to the shelter. It became very cramped when they joined us as well.

I fell asleep in the shelter. It must have been for some hours, even though the explosions continued for a while. All others had left when I awoke. I stepped outside. It was stunningly silent all around, at least there were no especially alarming sounds nearby. It was nothing like it had been in the morning, but there was buzzing in the air. My mother was sitting in the garden. Not in the late sunshine, but close to a wall and there was some overhead cover. It was about half past four, she told me. In the far distance we heard noises like fire exchanges. After four years of war they were rather familiar sounds. There was a big pit in a front garden at the lower end of our street- only five houses or so away from us.

Now what was going on and what was all this about?

Chapter Thirteen

Operation Market Garden –
More than an Assault

What was going on was Market Garden, an Allied military encounter between 17 and 26 September, 1944. The operation was the brainchild of Field Marshal Bernard L. Montgomery, commander of the 21 Army Group, comprising the British Second Army and the First Canadian Army. It involved simultaneous deployment of airborne troops and paratroopers as well as ground forces, aimed at taking several bridges in the Netherlands by surprise, to prevent them from being held or blown up by retreating German forces.

Market Garden actually intended to outflank the German *Westwall*, the major fortification between Cleves and Basel. It was about 630 km (390 miles) long. Jokingly called the Siegfried Line by the British, it was considered a major military obstacle in the summer of 1944. Montgomery next intended to enter the open North German Plain and conquer the Ruhr Territory, Germany's weapons forge.

The overall objective of Market Garden was to drive the German armed forces back to Berlin and to force an unconditional surrender. On the way, of course, it was also intended to liberate the Dutch people. The Allied ground forces were advancing rapidly in the summer of 1944, having landed in Normandy on D-Day back in June, but the bridges to achieve this additional goal had to be secured in a different way. Eijsden, Noorbeek and two more small Dutch towns were the first to be liberated, on 12 September 1944, by US First Army's 30 Infantry Division, known as 'Old Hickory' in honour of President Andrew Jackson. The Germans knew this unit as 'Roosevelt's SS'!

The US Ninth Army's 2nd Armoured Division, known as 'Hell on Wheels', entered nearby Maastricht two days later and took the city by the 16th. Six American GIs and a Frenchman, all scouts from 5th US Armoured Division, known as 'Victory', were the first Allies to enter Germany itself.

This happened on 11 September at Stolzembourg, near Vianden, in the Grand Duchy of Luxemburg. After having inspected the unmanned *Westwall* for two hours, they returned without being attacked.

Successive strategic bridges in the southeastern Netherlands, from North Belgium to Arnhem, were to be taken by parachute and airborne forces, while these forces were to be relieved by a simultaneous ground offensive. Arnhem was the furthest bridge for the Allies, but once it and the city were secured, it offered a direct advance into Germany, its Ruhr Territory, North Sea and Baltic Sea ports, and Berlin. Entering Germany in the autumn of 1944, bypassing the northern tip of the *Westwall*, Montgomery claimed that he believed he could 'end the war before Christmas'.

Montgomery found himself in a difficult position between Churchill, the British Prime Minister and Eisenhower, the Supreme Allied Commander in the West. At this point, Montgomery was far more optimistic than Eisenhower and had told Churchill many times that Allied troops could reach the borders of Germany by winter. This seems very optimistic since the original plans assumed an advance only to the Rhine by early 1946. There

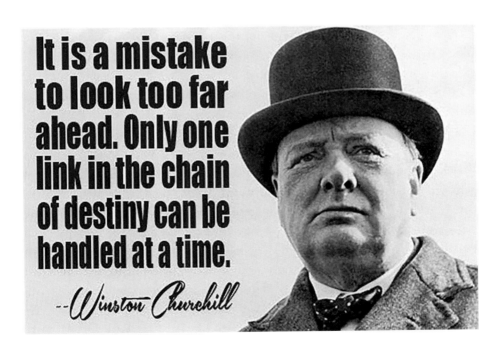

It is a mistake to look too far ahead. Only one link in the chain of destiny can be handled at a time.

-- Winston Churchill

were several verbal clashes between Montgomery and Eisenhower when the American had to remind the Englishman who was actually in command!

Market Garden proved that the advance across North Germany would be far from easy. At this stage, the Allies had one British airborne division and half a Polish brigade in the Arnhem area, and since this was the advance guard of Montgomery's Army Group, the German forces ranged against it were enormous.

Eisenhower did agree that bypassing the *Westwall's* north tip at Arnhem (securing the range of bridges) close on the Germans' retreating heels, was the best option at that moment. Meanwhile, because of the extreme length of supply lines through France as a result of the rapid advance, the Allies came to a standstill just short of the German border. This might enable the Germans to reassemble and offer more resistance. Montgomery was not the only commander who wanted more supplies in order to continue his advance. Generals Omar Bradley and George Patton were also making these demands, if anything more loudly and clearly! Eisenhower was on the horns of a dilemma.

The targets for Market Garden included several road and rail bridges on six major rivers and canals between Eindhoven and Arnhem. The city of Arnhem itself would be entered from the northeast, north and northwest. The Deelen air base was to be taken by two British infantry divisions. It had been hit by Allied bombing, but some anti-aircraft guns were still in place. The bridges to be taken between Eindhoven and Arnhem were 120km (72 miles) apart and the starting point was the bridge-head on the Kempisch Canal at Lommel, south of Eindhoven.

Viewed from south to north, the USAAF and two American airborne divisions were involved in ferrying and taking five major road bridges on rivers and canals between Eindhoven and Veghel. The 101st Airborne, the famous 'Screaming Eagles', operated at Grave and the 82nd, the 'All American' at Nijmegen. This operation included bridges over a canal between these cities, connecting the rivers Meuse and Waal. The sixth bridge in line was Arnhem's – there were actually two of them, road and rail, several kilometres apart, of which the road bridge was the more important.

The British 1st Airborne Division, the 'Red Devils', were flown directly to the Netherlands together with Polish forces. The Red Devils were commanded by Major-General Robert Urquhart, who lacked experience in this sort of warfare. Under him was Polish Major-General Sosabowski and his 1st Independent Polish Parachute Brigade. The road bridge at Arnhem was to be taken from both sides by British and Polish units.

American engineers were supposed to repair Deelen as a landing strip, in order to deploy three more infantry divisions and reinforce the battalions taking Arnhem and the bridge-head. Because of the speed of the German counter-attack, these repairs were not carried out and the divisions could not be deployed.

Field Marshal Bernard L. Montgomery, commander of the British 21st Army Group (comprising British 2nd Army and Canadian 1st Army) in 1944–45.

The objectives of Lieutenant General Brian Horrocks's XXX Army Corp in Market Garden were as follows: They were to relieve the airborne units on the bridges captured by the Allies and to reach Arnhem within three days.

All told, Market Garden was a very bold project indeed. Obviously, a ground force to be deployed from the Lommel area had to move fast, as it had to cover 120 km (72 miles) and relieve forces at bridges in enemy occupied country. The airborne forces were to be relieved as quickly as possible, certainly within three days of each other. It all had to work according to Montgomery's plan. There was little room for error – always tricky under

US General Dwight D. Eisenhower in 1944, Supreme Commander of the Allied Expeditionary Force (SHAEF) in Europe. A five-star general is the US Army's equivalent of a European field marshal.

war time conditions! The schedule was to take Eindhoven on the first day (Sunday, 17 September), Nijmegen on the next, Arnhem on the Tuesday, arriving there by 3pm. If anything went wrong at any of the bridges north of Eindhoven, then the result would be disaster. At the planning stage, no one could be sure where the greatest danger lay.

It was assumed that the Germans were on the brink of collapse after the battering they had taken since Normandy. This was a serious mistake. The Dutch believed that the Netherlands were about to be liberated. And they were wrong too. Lieutenant General Frederick 'Boy' Browning had his doubts about Market Garden and asked Montgomery if the project wasn't too audacious. He called Arnhem 'a bridge too far' and of course this assessment proved correct. Both he and Montgomery were criticised for their

Lieutenant General Brian G. Horrocks in 1945, commander of XXX Army Corps. He promised that his Corps would arrive in Arnhem 'in the same hours as 1st Airborne Division'.

decisions, but given the constraints of time there seemed to be little choice.

It is odd that, bearing in mind Browning's doubts, he should ignore the evidence provided not only by RAF photographs showing tanks in place, but also by the local Dutch Resistance, who were feeding him information. This Resistance unit was well organised, efficient, and free from German infiltration. It was a vital backup for the Allies throughout this entire period. Ignoring their advice led to the deployment of only one British division and one Polish brigade on the first and second days.

Montgomery brushed everyone's objections aside. He added that he had just received orders from London to eliminate the V-2 launch sites near The Hague, once Market Garden was concluded. It all added to the pressure Montgomery was under. This exchange of views took place just after

Major General Robert E. Urquhart, commander of the 1st Airborne Division, shown here at Hartenstein, Oosterbeek, in September 1944. When appointed, Urquhart had no airborne experience (he was prone to air-sickness) and was missing in Arnhem for two days after landing. However, he did not hesitate to do a sergeant's job, if necessary.

Lieutenant General Sir Miles C. Dempsey, commander of the Second Army in 1944–45.

10 September, nine days after Montgomery had been promoted to Field Marshal. Had this success gone to his head?

'A bridge too far' as a phrase has become commonly used in both the English and Dutch languages, including the United States and Belgium – the four countries involved most. A book with this title was published in Canada in 1948, although the 1975 book by Cornelius Ryan became better known, mainly because it was the basis of British producer Richard Attenborough's movie of 1977. The phrase now stands for any objective too ambitious to attain.

The aftermath of Market Garden was primarily a long lasting social tragedy for the people of Arnhem and for a number of towns such as Elst and Oosterbeek, and indeed for all Dutch families north of the Rhine. Some

Janny Bakker (8) at school in Eindhoven.

200,000 men, women, children may have been affected, mostly from Arnhem and to the west. After Market Garden, the Germans were fighting on their own soil and the attrition became more intense for the rest of the war. As with all countries occupied by the Germans, the Arnhem area suffered long after the fighting ceased.

Janny Bakker recalls the arrival of the first British ground forces in the north of the city, where she lived, on the 18th she thinks. As with most people, actual memories are strong, but when they happened is not always so clear.

'The British entered our street on foot, in their tanks and on trucks. People were wildly enthusiastic. Tanks were stopped and people put their kids on top of them, enabling them to enjoy a little ride! Many soldiers stayed until after the 18th for reasons we did not know, so they were offered rooms for the night. My parents did that, but the soldiers left their heavy trucks in the streets with engines running. There was a lot of noise, all through the nights.

They enjoyed their own meals which they prepared in our back yard. But several times in the next few days they prepared their meals for us as well. Which of course we appreciated very much after more than four years of scarcity. And those soldiers who had to stay in Eindhoven quickly seemed to enjoy being part of our family. One Sunday, as I remember, our house was so crowded with British soldiers that my parents decided not to go to church and attend worship.'

In other words, had there been fewer soldiers in the house, Janny's parents would have entrusted their house to the soldiers in order to attend worship.

It seemed those troops were set to occupy the city at least until the Germans were no longer a threat, while the real vanguard went on to the first bridge to be relieved. This was at Son, just north of Eindhoven. Janny recalls:

'They also offered blankets to us which were special in some way. We called them soldier blankets. And since textiles were very hard to get, my mother used one soldier blanket to sew a coat for me. A nice coat for the next winter.'

Along with their liberation, a new type of danger came to light. It is everywhere in the world to this day – unexploded devices left behind. They can be anywhere and are still recovered almost daily – not only in Germany, but throughout Europe. Janny recalls:

'One boy in our class-room found a grenade somewhere and picked it up. It exploded and the boy was killed instantly.'

He was certainly not the first boy in this country to lose his life, an arm or a leg, out of curiosity or an unhealthy interest in lost explosives.

'On one of the next days and also in the months to come', Janny says, 'I also offered my poetry album to the British soldiers'. This is something many young girls in their late 'zeros' and teens in the Netherlands owned since the end of the nineteenth century. The custom was to offer a small-sized album to someone they liked. It was an invitation to write something

Two pages of Janny's poetry album.

Lieutenant General Frederick A. 'Boy' Browning feared Arnhem was 'a bridge too far'.

nice and pleasant, and it was rude to refuse. One could write a (friendly) message, one could also write some well-known rhyme specially written for poetry albums. Stationers offered special stickers to dress up rhymes or messages in poetry-albums. Good looking young boys were presented with poetry albums frequently. After a week or so the album was returned, leaving the young owner with a lot of joy and surprise.

Janny had not been aware that poetry albums were unknown in Britain and that the soldiers barely understood what to do with them. Several did it their way and just wrote their names and some additional information, such as where they lived. Janny's father added the dates of the little entries.

A 22-year-old from Nijmegen, Jan van Hoof, is said to have saved the Waal River bridge on 18 September by cutting the wires between the switches and German charges placed under the bridge. Van Hoof was in a Resistance group which collected and reported military intelligence. He is said to have informed his sister on 18 September that 'the bridge is safe', but it is not clear what exactly he was referring to and what he actually did. There

Span of Nijmegen's Waal bridge.

were no witnesses to whatever actions Jan van Hoof undertook to save the bridge. On the 19th, he was seen guiding a British scout car in Nijmegen, sitting on top while waving a flag. The Germans fired and the two British soldiers inside the car were killed. Jan van Hoof was wounded, found to be a collaborator of the Allies, then beaten by the Germans and shot through his head. Legend about his share in having saved the bridge emerged soon after his death, probably just because the bridge remained intact.

My chief-editor in The Hague between 1970 and 1985, Jan van Beek, and his elder brother Marius lived in Nijmegen at the beginning of the war, like Van Hoof himself. Marius van Beek became a well-known sculptor in the Netherlands after the war. In 1940, when he was only nineteen, he had established a small Resistance group of which Van Hoof was a member. They had all known each other well before the war. The young daredevils used to have occasional drinks parties at Marius' home. Jan and Marius' mother was not pleased, however, when they laid their guns out on the table instead of keeping them hidden in their pockets. The group broke up abruptly in 1943, when Marius was wanted by the Germans. He immediately escaped to stay with relatives in his birthplace of Utrecht. He was sentenced to death in absentia. During this residence he became interested in the art of sculpture.

Marius' brother Jan, who was fifteen, had rushed to the city of Sittard in the south of the country when he heard that his brother was wanted, to avoid being taken hostage and shot instead – the Germans used to arrest a next of kin if they couldn't get the suspect they wanted. Jan was offered shelter with the Hermans family, unknown to him so far. After the war, one of the sons, Toon, became one of the most popular entertainers in the Netherlands for decades. Only after Market Garden and the liberation, did the Van Beek brothers return to Nijmegen.

Jan van Beek could speak German and English, so in 1945 he joined the British Liberation Army semi-officially, to serve as an interpreter and a road guide. He stayed with them as far as Bremen until the war was over. Van Hoof, who had not become a wanted man, had continued his Resistance work on behalf of 'London', by making sketches of intelligence targets in Nijmegen, until the time when he was killed. He was seen occasionally at the Waal River bridge.

After the war, Jan van Beek questioned the claims made by others about Van Hoof's actions, in a newspaper where he was employed as a young journalist. He did not question Van Hoof's intelligence gathering, but, as he told me later, 'he lacked military or technical know-how needed to deactivate charges'. He also called Van Hoof a 'modest young man, not the daredevil kind who would spring into action like this'. Jan's elder brother disagreed with him.

According to Marius's son Michael, speaking in November 2015, Marius had always been convinced that Van Hoof really had cut the wires, which of course is not really the same as deactivating the charges. It is even claimed that Bittrich defied Model's order not to blow-up the bridge, but due to a mystery fault the bridge remained intact. Messrs. Jan and Marius are no

British Liberation Army soldiers Miller and Jones. The discs are German 'Teller Mines', or disc mines.

longer with us. 'Marius used to become irritated when someone questioned Jan van Hoof's cutting of the wires', Michael says, so Marius was convinced of Van Hoof's Resistance act. While, according to Jan van Beek's widow, Margreet, Marius told his brother in private that he did not believe that Van Hoof had cut the wires. Marius also claimed that other members of this former Resistance group doubted that Jan van Hoof could have cut the wires. One day, according to Margreet, Jan and Marius decided never again to discuss the Van Hoof matter to avoid needless heated discussions.

An official Dutch investigation after the war found no proof that Jan van Hoof either cut the wires, or deactivated the charges. It is likely that the question wasn't actually relevant anyway, as Model had ordered that the bridges of Arnhem and Nijmegen be saved and not blown up. The Dutch

Sherman tanks rolling north along the Waal River bridge, Nijmegen, on 20 September 1944. The debris on the pavement are the remnants of deactivated German mines. Such clearance was necessary as the Germans made several attempts to destroy the bridge over the following days, but were unsuccessful. The arch, built in 1936, can still be seen over the river today.

investigation confirmed this when it discovered that 'they [the Germans] did not execute the destruction of the bridge on the basis of orders given at the time'. These would have been Model's orders. In fact, the wires were cut by two British soldiers from the Coldstream Guards Armoured Division.

One of the Guards was an 'impressive and smart' Corporal Miller who is not famous for any other actions; the other was Sapper Tony Jones, who were both in the same squad as Robert Boscawen, who is author of the book *Armoured Guardsman* (Pen & Sword, 2001). To quote Boscawen, 'The former [Sapper Jones] was to cut the wires and immobilize the extensive demolition charges under and above the huge Nijmegen bridge and so helped to open the final stage in the ill-fated battle to relieve our airborne forces at Arnhem'. Unfortunately, they were too late to achieve that final and most crucial objective.

There is a surprising monument to this public controversy. The civic leaders in Nijmegen wanted a local hero and commissioned Marius van Beek to create a bronze sculpture, to honour Jan van Hoof's doubtful action. This bronze sculpture of a man in 1944 carrying a flag was unveiled in a widely attended ceremony in 1954. The ambassadors of the USA, the UK and Canada were present. The sculpture is situated prominently at the south end of the Waal River bridge on a roundabout, making Jan van Hoof a well-known person in Dutch war time history and honouring a hero who probably wasn't one at all.

Chapter Fourteen

Liberation at the Doorstep

The real start of the operation in the southeastern Netherlands took place on the afternoon of 17 September 1944. It was another big surprise for those located on the long perimeter between the Belgian border and Arnhem, as far as along as Ginkel Heath. There were bombings around noon and then after 2.00pm, many thousands of paratroops jumped from Dakotas, slightly modified Halifaxes, Stirlings and other transport planes, while field guns fired and ground forces rumbled north. There were thousands of parachutists, all the way from Eindhoven to the Arnhem area. It was some sight!

Gerrit Lourens remembers:

The spectacular sight of parachuted divisions during Market Garden. This original photograph shows Ginkel Heath, between Ede and Arnhem.

'In the afternoon we witnessed a spectacle like never before. The planes were flying very low [towards the landing zones] with gliders in tow. As we understood later, these Horsa gliders carried jeeps, 75 mm anti-tank guns, mortars, machine guns and bren carriers. [As much as maximum take-off weight permitted, they also took airborne troops and their armaments]. We stood outside and watched all these planes breathlessly. Many tow-ropes were detached just above our heads. The gliders then came down about 2 or 3 kilometres [1.5 miles] in front of us [landing and dropping in zone 'X'] for what usually was a rough landing. Not a single plane was shot down, although some gliders overturned and crashed.'

Close to Arnhem however, at Landing zone 'L' maybe, seven gliders were hit by German Flak.

Gerrit continues:

'We could see all this perfectly, since rye in a field behind the houses in front of us had been collected a few weeks before. Yes, summer rye is not the finest. But there was a war on, remember? One tow-rope detached both from a towing plane and the glider. It landed on a roof across the street and even though it was nylon, the rope caused a big hole in the roof. After the gliders came the paratroopers. Hundreds, thousands of them. We found out later that they were the Red Devils from the colours of their berets. Next to the paratroopers there were parachutes in different colours with different kinds of supplies. Like ammo, penicillin, medicaments, food. Many chutes were clear red and clear green. Paratroopers however were hanging on army green chutes. Against the backdrop of a clear blue sky and watching them from the south, it was a sight to behold really. Overwhelming. My mother managed to find one of those chutes and made a shirt of it for me. We could still use the rope many years later.'

Nasty experiences in the enemy-held territory were inevitable. Many paratroopers landed at Ginkel Heath, just as a detachment of mixed German and Dutch SS marched to Arnhem from their partly bombed Ede barracks.

Instantly, they started firing at the Many paratroopers, who in very many cases still were hanging in mid-air. These scenes were witnessed by many spectators who watched the breath-taking landings from great distances. SS men had gained a reputation of killing POWs since 1939, but 'in their minds this firing at soldiers in mid-air was even *more fun*', Gerrit adds in a sour voice. 'They wounded the British, killed them, shot the chutes on fire so that the soldiers smashed themselves up, and on top of that, took photos and movies of their deeds.' We know this, as the movie images are in Dutch archives today.

Caroline, another youngster from those days, recalled:

'When the shooting was interrupted, wherever it came from, we left our basement, took to the street and were very surprised to see the airborne landings in the west, over Oosterbeek and even further away. Hundreds of planes continued to fly into the distance. There was no end to the sound of their humming, while hundreds and hundreds of parachutists continued to jump out of the aircraft. Yes, of course we asked our parents what it was all about. We may have seen parachutists before, but in such cases, only jumping from one aircraft. This time it was so different. The planes dropped the paras, then turned away instead of crashing to the ground. Altogether, it was such a beautiful spectacle, all those hundreds of puppets hanging on their chutes, hovering in mid-air, coming down slowly. We were convinced we would be free within a few days. We shouted with joy and jumped up and down in front of our houses.

'But from across the street, we were made clear to be careful. "They are not here," the man who lived there said. True, the parachutists were landing, but they were not actually in our area. This brought us back to reality. Besides, this man was known to be sympathetic to the Germans. We had to be careful.'

At the same time, several Many paratroopers remembered that while hanging on their chutes, they noticed Arnhem in the distance and were surprised by the size of a city most had never heard of before. Similarly, Frost's battalion were similarly surprised when they noticed the height of the Rhine bridge they were to seize in the next hour or so. That is, once they were in the streets quite near the bridge. As explained, the bridge was built to give clearance to Rhine barges, a larger kind of barge, taller usually and powered by sails much larger than comparable sails on other rivers and canals, before 1940. When unrestricted Rhine shipping was allowed again by the occupying authorities in 1948, sails gave way to bigger and taller motor barges.

Meanwhile Caroline's father – like thousands of others – viewed the same endless stream of transports and thousands of parachutists jumping from them, from his Arnhem house. This was at least 15km (9 miles) away. Like so many others then, he kept a diary in which he later wrote:

'When the Germans had recovered from the initial shock of the operation, the spectacle became less attractive, as they fired at the planes. Some gliders crash-landed. But parachutists were hit as well and smashed to the ground with their parachutes burning.'

His 7-year-old son Paul, younger brother to Caroline and John, remembered the same – soldiers hanging on burning chutes. He just stood at the front door of his house watching. He was appalled and referred back to the cruel scenes of smoking and burning chutes time and again when the war was over. And when asked today, he still does. Our niece, Plien, could also clearly see the paratroopers landing and she was in in Velp – a distance of 20 km (12 miles) at least.

Paul, Caroline, John and Plien were just four youngsters out of many thousands of spectators of all ages in a large area around the landings. Then what about me? I was hardly any further from the spectacle than Paul. I saw nothing of it on 17 September. It is fair to assume that I was asleep in the shelter in our back yard. My parents also missed some of the spectacle, as there were many houses as well as tall beech trees preventing a clear view of what was happening out to the west. But my father knew something was going on one way or another, by the many plane engines and other loud noises, ack-ack guns for example, that he could hear. He went down the street to the arterial Velperweg and joined others to watch the exceptional events in the air. And since, in this part of the country, many people enjoy the strange habit of joining in with strangers' conversations, he quickly had gained a picture of what was going on.

Back at Renkum, much closer to the scene with Gerrit again:

'Surely our liberation was near, but knowing the Germans, we were also sure that intense fighting was inevitable before it was achieved.'

Up until that moment, few Germans had been seen in Renkum – in fact at some points there were none there at all. This time it was different. Gerrit continues:

'For our safety, we decided to sleep in the basement since we heard gunfire in our area. Germans had surrounded the dropping and landing zones. Even so, we saw and heard Allied transports bringing more paras and supplies. It was only after some days that quiet returned to the air. We were allowed to go out for some shopping, mostly because the schools were closed for safety reasons. As an 11-year-old, I started to investigate our area. Behind a wall, I was surprised to find a dead German soldier, killed in action. He was surrounded by many empty gun shells. I collected those shells and mumbled: *You nasty Jerry!*, while I kicked his ass. No, I have never regretted this ever.'

Once the air landings near Arnhem were assessed, the Germans needed little time or imagination to determine what steps were to be taken, where to assemble their troops and where to set up counter-attacks. There were many different combat units in the area and most knew the area well, whilst the British carried old, out-of-date maps. The Germans were able to use some tracks and roads the British had no chance of knowing about. This was much like the old radio equipment they carried. The radios didn't work at all at any range. As a consequence, units near Arnhem were unable to communicate with each other, with their command in Britain (FAAA), or with Browning.

Regardless of this, the Dutch welcomed the British very enthusiastically. They were cheered, embraced, showered with presents including fruit and small orange banners. It was impossible for the troops to ignore this and it all caused delay. Even though the Dutch in their unrestricted enthusiasm were not very different from so many others in Western Europe, this delay cost precious hours and lives.

Between 7.30 and 8pm on this historic Sunday, Frost and his battalion entered Arnhem's *Markt* which borders the fifteenth-century Eusebius Tower and Church. Both are massive landmarks. The complex is one of the best decorated in the country and Arnhemers take much pride in it. The tower was 85m (279ft) tall.

My 68-year-old grandfather, Harm Kuiper, was one of those to witness the British advance at the *Markt*. He and his wife lived alongside his bakery business, in a seventeenth-century building, in the oldest district of the city, in a street running off the *Markt*. Grandad was not of a timid nature. He stepped outside into the *Markt* out of curiosity when he saw soldiers in unfamiliar uniforms and suddenly heard gunfire. He had some sort of conversation with Frost's men – a short conversation for sure. They were heading for the nearby bridge before it might be too far.

Grandad ignored the German bullets raining down. He was somewhat reticent and never used to making much fuss, but he did write later that he 'Shook hands with the English'. This was a slightly different reaction to the great enthusiasm of others in other places, but he did it nonetheless. He also noted several unusual sounds and events in the streets around him, at the *Markt* when he went out, as well as in the Turfstraat where he lived in the front part of the house. The rear of his house was the bakery which opened onto the curve of another street, just below the Eusebius tower. This street was actually officially called 'Behind the Tower', although it was in front of the tower.

There were more unusual incidents on that Sunday evening. Germans were shooting from a safe spot – which just happened to be the open door of grandad's bakery – towards the *Markt*, until they were spotted by one or perhaps a few British soldiers. These soldiers were in the parallel Turfstraat on the other side of the house. They became aware of the Germans when they looked through an open door inside the house. Both parties started firing at each other almost instantly, right through grandad's house, shattering his windows, furniture and what have you. The damage done to the house, the shop and the danger to himself and his wife compelled grandad to intervene. He approached each side and made clear, most likely in angry Dutch and waving his hands, probably with a finger pointing at the guns, his windows and maybe his head as well: 'Listen, we have not been to bed last night. But we want you to stop the firing through my house, as we want to go to bed now.' Market Garden or not, it was his belief that they should stop. Amazingly, it worked.

Frost's men, meanwhile, did not join Major Gouch's reconnaisance group which was supposed to have arrived there, unaware that the group had not been able to reach the bridge. But a few men had managed to reach the *Markt* on their own. Out of the original four crossings of the Rhine, this high road bridge then was Frost's very last opportunity to make Market Garden a success – but only if Horrocks' tanks could relieve Frost in time. Their first step was to occupy a few buildings next to the north ramp of the bridge. Once on the bridge, they tried to reach the other, southern ramp. This failed, due to heavy German fire. It was not a holiday trip, after all! In view of the size of his battalion, it became clear to Frost that his men could not take the entire bridge.

Grandad's Kuiper's remark in his diary, the 'English' had taken the bridge, therefore was not entirely correct. It showed more enthusiasm than he could justify. But what he observed at the *Markt* and even inside his own house, was very clear. Grandad's diary next says:

> 'Watched some German POWs at the Markt on Monday morning. Many fire exchanges by noon. Even more in the evening. Germans coming from [nearby] Baker Street entering my bakery with heavy machine gun. Heavy shooting towards the Markt. Shooting also down from the Eusebius Church. Tiles and rubble from neighbouring houses on our roof.'

SS Captain Viktor Graebner enjoyed a reputation for always following his own initiative. When he decided to returned to Arnhem from Elst on Monday, he took twenty-two of his forty vehicles with him. There was only one direct road between Nijmegen and Arnhem in 1944, so Graebner was trapped. Thus, he decided to return and destroy the British on the Arnhem bridge. It had to be relieved by XXX Corps as soon as possible. German mines in Arnhem were in place, but not connected and never used.

Graebner's approach of the Rhine bridge on the next morning was noticed by Frost's battalion. The British had hoped that they were Horrocks' force. But, as a precaution, they had also laid mines on the road. A few of the German vehicles managed to escape damage by zigzagging around the mines. Once it was clear that they were German vehicles, the British opened heavy fire on the next wave of vehicles from the buildings on both sides of the north ramp. This would have been what my grandfather heard and commented on in his diary, 'many fire exchanges by noon'. Twelve vehicles were destroyed by mines and British fire. Over seventy Germans were killed in a two hour fight, including captain Viktor Graebner. This scene became part of the movie *A Bridge Too Far*.

Grandad also noticed German POWs on the *Markt* on Monday. It would not have taken long for them to be captured. The conditions that the men were fighting in were most unusual of course, being in a rather rural provincial capital like Arnhem, especially when German vehicles came under heavy British fire on the bridge. At the same time these conditions prevented my own father from leaving home to start work in the bakery or take care of his parents; he faced streets blocked by policemen.

Grandad and his wife (whom he married after my father's mother had died in the early 1920s) had stayed on the ground floor, at street level of their house and bakery, although there was a basement. Staying at street level enabled him to see in part what was happening outside.

'Monday evening', he noted, 'fire at the house of the Queen's Commisioner [the first authority in any province] at the Markt. The house which also is his cabinet [office] burnt down, including some neighbouring houses. Sunday night to Monday morning to bed from 04.00 to 06.00am only. Monday to Tuesday not to bed. Joined by terrified unknown young couple seeking shelter with us after escape from their house that was ablaze at the Markt. Neighbours opposite our house fled on Monday because of fire, which was extinguished by one of their next door neighbours. All night shooting and Germans everywhere now.'

Their own neighbours meanwhile believed all this was far too dangerous for the elderly couple and they also felt grandad was more curious than was good for him. But how did they know? Chances are that they came by to purchase some bread. Grandad wrote:

> 'On the repeated urgings of our neighbours [we went to] the basement on Tuesday morning, about 11.00am. This day was most frightening and dangerous. Fire in the Court of Justice complex across the Markt. Entirely burnt out.'

The front of the complex had four Roman-style columns. One of them was broken half way up. It was removed in 1945 to become the official monument of the Battle of Arnhem. It is situated nearby at the lower end of the Rhine bridge and it is there where the annual commemorations take place.

> 'Next ablaze were the Tax-offices, House of Detention [which was part of the Court of Justice complex], the Roman-Catholic St. Walburgis church nearby [Arnhem's oldest church, built in the middle of the fourteenth century], as well as Insula Dei hospital [which had been hit by a bomb on Sunday, two days earlier, and evacuated].'

Of all these buildings, only the outer walls of the church and its twin towers were to survive the war, even after a German fighter plane flying too low had hit a tower in heavy fog in November – the pilot being killed on impact. My grandfather did not see this incident. He continues in his diary:

> 'About 3.00pm a heavy piece of artillery was placed in the Markt, just at the top of our street. It was only fired two or three times, but in the basement we could hear our windows rattle. A German soldier came down to our basement during a pause in fighting two hours later and told us that we could leave the house safely. It was, in fact, an order. We left the basement to prepare tea and collect some vital supplies, but we ignored the order to leave.
>
> 'It was hard to do that though, as there was much debris cascading down from the church. Unlike ours, there was much damage to our neighbour's house. Fortunately, most of our upper story windows were

still intact. So we made ourselves tea first and started packing our supplies. Heavy fire then resumed so we returned to the basement.'

Grandad and his wife, both about the same age, were not at all convinced that they were in danger, although the firing in the area around the bridge and the *Markt* reached their peak during that evening of Tuesday. But that same evening, Germans entered during a short pause in the fighting. They ordered them to come out of the basement and leave the house immediately. The couple decided to go this time, but he forgot to take his savings with him from his money box in the basement. In it were banknotes and silver coins. It was a fair amount of money which he had been putting aside over the years as a retirement pension.

In Arnhem there were two separate places where the fighting continued (apart from individual soldiers who had lost contact with their units). Next to the bridge and the neighbouring *Markt* area, there was heavy fighting near Elisabeth's hospital in the west end of the city and at the cross roads of five streets a little further on. Tanks from the 10 SS Frundsberg Division participated in this street fighting. On the British side, there were isolated battles. Failing radio communication was one thing, but much more was going wrong for the British, who invariably had the sympathy and support of the Dutch. The most important problem was that Horrocks' XXX Corps did not show up to relieve them. Additionally, while Urquhart was 'missing' for some days, Lathbury was heavily wounded in his spine and a leg.

The heavy tanks of the Frundsberg Division, looking battered, had passed the Velperweg crossroad on our street on their way to the west side of Arnhem on Tuesday. They had arrived from the northeast. Their colour was a sandy yellow. Tanks in the streets were exceptional. I stood there for a while, watching the long row of different types of vehicles passing by at high speed, until my mother found me. She had heard the noise as well. She was far from happy to see me standing down the street. The tanks and other tracked vehicles all made such a strange, unfamiliar impression on me, I told her. Watching tanks while down in the city while a war was on! Was I out of my mind?! She grabbed me by the arm and pulled me home. 'And you will stay at home. Is that understood?' It is true, the sounds of heavy fighting downtown could clearly be heard in our district.

Meanwhile my father and his eldest brother Johan, Caroline's father, were very worried about their own parents at Turfstraat. From quite a distance they could see the spire of the Eusebius in smoke and flames. My father was very shocked. Like many in the city, he really loved the high Eusebius tower. As both his brothers and two sisters were born in Turfstraat, they trembled at the fate of their parents. Explosions from that part of the city near the bridge could clearly be heard. The two brothers decided to cycle there. But they were halted by local police and Germans. No entry. It was a combat zone, perilous for any civilian. The British were fighting against tanks at the lower end of the bridge, with only hand weapons. The brothers had no choice but to return. The explosions and the billowing smoke at several places made them fear the worst about their parents.

Elsewhere in the city centre, one tank was positioned at Steenstraat which was on the edge of the city. The crew fired at the top floor of the national department store called V&D (equivalent to Marks and Spencer) at the opposite end of the square. Once the top floor was ablaze, the next floor down was their target until the entire building was completely destroyed. It did not take very much time. Germans around the tank were asked by Dutch spectators what the purpose was of this deliberate, useless destruction of a department store. It was needed to prevent British snipers from taking position on top of the store, they said. To that end a German tank had broken into the store just before the shooting. But there weren't any British in that part of the centre! The Germans knew that. It was just prevention. It looked more like a training crew exercise. It was typical German reasoning, not much different from the way they treated much of the rest of the city's buildings in the months to come.

My grandparents certainly were not the first to escape from the houses in their street on that Tuesday night. The continuous battles, bullets flying around, explosions everywhere, fires, and the danger of being unable to survive the ordeal at all had led others to flee. They were not the first civilians to escape from the centre of Arnhem or the Oosterbeek area, as there was continuous fighting there as well. At one moment, there was just about fighting everywhere in the area around the Rhine bridge and all the way west. My grandparents were suddenly ordered to go in the direction the Germans pointed; like refugees without a choice.

They had no idea where to go. They were not evacuees, as the Germans put it, since there was no chance of returning in the foreseeable future and there was not a single refugee centre. My grandfather and his wife left behind all their private and business possessions and were among the first in Arnhem in 1944 to lose everything. This even included their pet parakeet called Piet, left behind in his cage (though my cousin Paul always claimed it was a canary). Once in the street, they dashed from one doorway to the next, amidst thunderous noise, whizzing bullets, explosions, fires, and the screaming of fighting and wounded soldiers.

The exception to all this damage was Grandad's own house. As he crossed the street to take one last look at his beloved home, the last of his life, he saw his wide, four storey seventeenth-century house still standing with much

When Arnhem's electricity cut out on 17 September, all twenty-five trams in service at that time stopped for good. This photograph was taken where *Bovenover* street (front) and *Onderlangs* (left, not visible) joined. All other tram cars were in the depot, which was destroyed during the battle. Here, German tanks are seen heading west on the Tuesday or Wednesday. The photograph was taken by a German army photographer. (*Coll. Neth. Institute for Military History, The Hague*)

less damage than he had expected. Even most of the windows remained unbroken. Then my poor grandparents had to make their way over all kinds of litter, rubble, burning partly collapsing houses, to get out of their street and out of the city's centre. Around the corner more houses were ablaze. And more people were fleeing their homes, which in most cases were flats above shops. They all managed to reach the border of the city's centre.

Naturally, the elderly couple were welcome with any of their three sons. But either grandad did not consider going to one of his sons, or it was just impossible to reach them at that time. At Willems Square, they had to manoeuvre around a great number of tanks with their engines running, ready to roll in any direction. The couple headed to relatives living in a street at the north side of the railway. Once underneath the railway viaduct, they were nearly there and safe, as they had covered the most dangerous 900m (3,000ft) of their lives. It was very fortunate that both enjoyed good health, and were not suffering from a heart condition, or some other illness of old age. Although the relatives were not expecting to see grandad and his wife, they were warmly welcomed and very pleased to be given their first good hot meal in a number of shocking days. Only the next day, Wednesday, did they have an opportunity to inform their sons that they were safe.

Grandad's middle son, Carel, urged the couple to come to him as soon as they possibly could. Carel, who lived at Velp with his wife and two daughters, also owned a bakery. It was in a separate building next to his home. He lived in a large house with many rooms. As a matter of fact, he had offered shelter to his parents-in-law already, who also had escaped from Arnhem. They came from just as dangerous a street in the centre. Offering shelter was Carel's second nature, particularly now that people had to rely on each other even more than they had before. Families had to take care of one another. Social welfare and state retirement pensions barely existed during the war. On the other hand, very many local governments (and companies) had a lot of cash, because, during the war, there was little opportunity of investing in anything. Many city councils could afford to offer help and acted accordingly in the months to come.

The family asked grandad Harm and his wife to recall their experiences of the last three days, while Carel was able to tell them what was going on from a broader point of view. Carel was much amused when his father told him how he had reacted to both the British and the German soldiers firing through his house. He told his father to write it all down, but grandad had left his diary behind. So he started another for their most recent experiences. As grandad and his wife stayed with Carel until after the end of the war, he kept the diary with him and it has survived. The story of the shooting through the house and the night's rest they did not want to miss became the family joke when the war was over.

Chapter Fifteen

A Heart Attack for Hitler

S Obergruppenfüehrer Bittrich had taken several major steps on 17 September as soon as the Luftwaffe informed him about Allied airborne landings near Arnhem and Nijmegen. Bittrich was one German officer able to react fast and produce several combat units when a counter-attack was needed. Just like other commanders, he assembled combat units literally from everywhere on 17 September and the days after, and even included clerks, cooks and military patients recovering in hospitals. He didn't care if they were Luftwaffe or Kriegsmarine personnel. This undermined the Germans' reputation as Prussian bureaucrats and underscored the way they were trained.

Bittrich's divisional HQ was at Doetinchem, 27km (16 miles) east of Arnhem as the crow flies. Men on leave were recalled, any armoured vehicles and equipment that were ready or on their way to Germany for repair was to be unloaded from the freight trains that were transporting them, and any that had reached Germany had to be returned. He ordered his subordinates Walter Harzer and Heinz Harmel into action with their much depleted 9th Hohenstaufen and 10th Frundsberg Tank divisions respectively. Harmel happened to be in Berlin acquiring new tanks (his were all lost in Normandy) and was in greater need of reinforcements. He returned to Arnhem immediately when notified of what was going on there. Apart from his men, he could deploy only tracked and armoured vehicles.

Harzer who was not yet thirty-two years old, was ordered to prepare one combat unit and head for the landing areas at Oosterbeek 'to annihilate the enemy troops which have landed. It is essential to strike immediately,' Bittrich commanded, 'whilst it is also urgent to occupy and secure the (Arnhem Rhine) bridge with strong forces.' The real size of this fighting unit is hard to gauge as available figures differ widely. There could have been several thousand men. They faced Lieutenant Colonel Fitch's 3rd Battalion first.

In view of Harmel's return, Bittrich ordered 10th Frundsberg Division to head for Nijmegen and create a bridgehead with available vehicles to prevent a breakthrough of the XXX Army Corps. If Bittrich wasn't informed of this British advance, he could easily second guess it, following German practice in the Netherlands in 1940 and Allied practice later. The Frundsberg forces and vehicles, however, were quartered many kilometres northeast of Arnhem, in the Deventer area, which is also northwest of the town of Doetinchem. They were detailed to recapture Nijmegen's road bridge on the Waal River if captured by the Allies. This was not the case on the evening of 17 September. An American platoon was near the bridge in the city, but not on the bridge. Few Germans were on the bridge, but this changed quickly.

Bittrich could not use the public telephone lines to issue his orders to Arnhem, as other Germans had been ordered to close virtually all telephone communication. So, he put an orderly on a bike and sent him to Arnhem, ordering Harzer to send a reconnaissance unit to Nijmegen. The distance from Doetinchem was 40km (25 miles) including a time-consuming river crossing, while the last part was steeply uphill over the Arnhem hills. It took an hour and a half for him to arrive at Harzer's barracks in Arnhem. Fortunately the order was written, as the orderly was out of breath upon arrival and unable to speak coherently.

Bittrich and Harzer assessed the situation and issued orders while Colonel Frost's 2nd Battalion had marched into Arnhem. They captured the north ramp of the road bridge next. They prevented Harzer and his Frundsberg division from entering the Rhine bridge to head south for Nijmegen. Gunshots ensued immediately in the twilight.

Planting their feet on the bridge was a historic triumph and the rumour that 'British airborne troops had taken the bridge' quickly spread through Arnhem and Oosterbeek. Unfortunately, it was a short-lived and only partial triumph and yet its fame has survived all other disputed events, disgraces and circumstances in the week to come. It is the triumph for which the road bridge of Arnhem has borne John Frost's name since 16 September 1978, even though he was reluctant for this to happen – for obvious reasons. Frost's men arrived at the bridge shortly after Graebner and his reconnaissance force of forty tracked and armoured vehicles had crossed it. They were ordered to size up the situation at the Waal bridge in Nijmegen. Graebner did not encounter Frost. As this bridge was the final part of Operation Market, the most intense single battle ever to take place in the Netherlands, it seems inevitable that the name of John Frost (on behalf of his battalion) will never disappear from the Arnhem road bridge on the Rhine.

Meanwhile there was another German battalion, camping out in the wooded areas of Wolfheze. This was SS Lieutenant Colonel Sepp Krafft's well-organised unit of some 430 very young men. It was a training unit, comprising fanatic German boys mainly aged 17 to 19 years old. Like Spindler, Krafft was ordered by Harzer to move into position and prevent any British advances from their landing areas towards Arnhem. These youngsters, who had been in Arnhem since 4 September, may very well have been the ones which annoyed my mother so much. We were out in the city centre one day, when she indicated with a nod of her head to a column of very young looking soldiers marching along and singing a soldier's song loudly.

'Too young,' was what my mother thought. Warriors with somewhat high, unmartial voices. She was talking about 16-year-old boys. There was nothing 'young' about them in my eyes, but then I was only about 5. These youngsters had just been promoted from the Hitler Youth, and were part of Hitler's '*letztes Aufgebot*', as it was called, some of the Füehrer's 'final reserves'. Krafft carried out Harzer's order quickly and efficiently by blocking most main roads into Arnhem, thus delaying the advancing paratroopers earlier than they may have expected. Besides and as a surprise, the Germans threw their 7th Parachute Division into the battle. It had only been formed in mid-August.

This was not all. As well as these so-called last reserves, Harzer deployed a battalion of armoured grenadiers against the paratroopers and airborne troops. These were young enlisted infantry, which had existed as a force since 1942. When taken to the front lines, they were mounted on tracked vehicles – *Aufgesessen* as the Germans called it. When facing battle, they went on as infantry. Their combat duties interfered with the deployment of the light tanks and vehicles. The battalion was deployed on 17 September to cover a few rural roads outside Arnhem and cut off British forces before marching into Arnhem. These mounted grenadiers were enforced by still another combat unit, most likely Spindler's.

'*Aufgesessen*' German tank or armoured grenadiers in Russia. (*Bundesarchiv Picture 183-J14778*)

Harzer ordered yet another battalion of armoured grenadiers to the bridge. His orders were to: break British resistance and recapture the north ramp of the bridge on the city side; prevent the passage of reinforcements from the landing zones west of Oosterbeek to the bridge; encircle British troops at the bridge and destroy them as soon as reinforcements arrived. Many more German forces in the Netherlands were available. Commanders of various tank units informed Luftwaffe General Friedrich Christiansen, the Wehrmacht's supreme commander in the Netherlands, that they were available to help. Lieutenant General Hans von Tettau also volunteered his services. He was a manager of the SS school in Arnhem and his office was in Hilversum. An unspecified number of Henschel-produced Tiger II tanks, 80-ton monsters named after Bengal tigers (called king tigers in German), were sent from Germany in the course of the week in support of the SS tank division remnants in the Arnhem area.

General Bittrich then applied for troops, armour and tanks from Army Group B. Model sent infantry battalions experienced in street combat, artillery to be positioned on Arnhem's high ground, a brigade of Flak and a unit of heavy Tiger tanks with Krupp guns. Early on the morning of 18 September, orders for action were issued to one artillery regiment, two infantry regiments, as well as a tank unit of these formidable King Tiger tanks, a few smaller battalions such as the pioneers experienced in flame throwing, the police and the so-called *Landsturm* (soldiers). At sunrise all these forces headed for Arnhem. It is hard to say how many men and how much equipment were involved in all this. Among them however were those SS-units which marched on the road from Ede towards Arnhem while more British paratroopers landed on 18 September, and shot them while they still hung on their chutes. The Dutch saw this widely observed incident as shocking and another example of the bestiality of the SS.

Finally, as far as the Arnhem area was concerned, the German 116th Tank Division was sent to the Betuwe to operate near Driel. Deployment of this Division near Arnhem is not well-known generally, but it is confirmed in a few books of recent years. One such confirmation is by a German veteran in a Dutch book called *Wegmoffelen* by Ingrid Maan of Oosterbeek (2015). This Division had operated in Normandy to facilitate the escape of Germans from the Falaise Pocket, although not unscathed. Only 600 infantry and 12 tanks were saved. These remnants were transferred to the Aachen area and then deployed in the Netherlands. They faced the Polish battalion near Driel.

Kurt Student was ordered by Model to 'defend' Eindhoven, to which end this city was to be retaken by the Germans from east and west first. Model's command promised also to deploy a Wehrmacht Infantry division in the Eindhoven area, as well as a tank division, against the 101. Infantry-General Gustav von Zangen's 15th Army of 150,000 men, who attacked US troops in Eindhoven from 17 to 27 September. German numbers were overwhelmingly superior but were not successful and Eindhoven was not retaken. There was no deployment of the *Kriegsmarine* in the Netherlands, just as in 1940.

When Adolf Hitler was informed about Market Garden, late that Sunday, he threw a fit of anger and then had a heart attack. This is quoted in *Chronik 1944 Tag fuer Tag in Wort und Bild* published by Bertelsmann, in Guetersloh in 1988. It is a series that takes Germany's twentieth century history one year per volume and is written and produced to look like a daily newspaper:

'When Hitler is told about the Allied air landing at Arnhem on 17 September, he suffers from a heart attack. Much weakened, in an apathetic mood and not wanting to live, he lies down on a bed for hours and then is also struck by sinusitis.'

Bertelsmann earned millions during the war as it was the biggest single publisher of Nazi propaganda.

Things with the Füehrer were serious.

'Hitler's physical decline', the report continued, 'can no longer be stopped. On 1 October (1944) he loses consciousness for a short time. Thereafter his condition continues to deteriorate (…)'

Hitler had been informed that an Allied offensive was to be expected very soon. The citizens of Arnhem, however, had never been aware how dear they and their city were to the Füehrer, as the news of Market Garden led to his reported heart attack far away in East Prussia.

The Führer took over twenty-five drugs per day in those sunset months until they were no longer needed in 1945. There were pills, injections, drops and vitamins, prescribed to him by Theodor Morell. Morrell had been Hitler's physician since the mid-thirties. One of the medicines was called mutaflor, and was said to be developed by Morell himself in 1936, to deal with Hitler's flatulence which had been caused by the drug taking. Dr. Morell was taken prisoner by American forces in 1945 and kept in custody in Buchenwald. He was not charged with anything criminal as there was no longer any evidence of the Füehrer's digestive problems and he was released. Compared to the fact that designer Hugo Boss was fined DM 100,000 (US$ 70,500 at the time) for having designed and produced all Nazi uniforms, this seems strange.

The *Chronik 1944* entry, written after the war, led with a feature about the decline of Hitler's health since 1941. The man's health had never been good. It might have been even worse for him and his political ambitions if he had been wounded more seriously during the First World War. He suffered two injuries and hospitalization, but nothing serious like his jaw being shot away or his right arm being crushed as happened to so many other soldiers at the time. His will power to achieve political targets has been likened to 'a volcano'. Such an explosive nature can lead to simple heart attacks, although that doesn't always follow. Hitler's stressful life during the war may have caused sufficient tension to make us believe that his health took a serious turn in the autumn of 1944. Hitler truly was 'a dying scorpion' as at least one British writer said.

Hitler was not in Berlin, but in his East Prussian hideout called *Wolfschanze* (the Wolf's Lair), when the news about Arnhem was given to him. Hours after his outburst of anger and collapse, he decided that fighting the Allied troops in the Arnhem area was top priority. As a first step, he made Luftwaffe units comprising 300 fighter planes available to Model. They operated from ten different bases in the Ruhr area and carried out many attacks on Allied forces heading for, or fighting all the way to Arnhem.

Hans Dietr Student, son of Kurt Student was one of the Luftwaffe pilots deployed. He was in a squadron fighting from the Ruhr bases, three of which were Dortmund, Paderborn and Guetersloh. His squadron was heavily involved in attacking Allied planes with tactical strafing during Market Garden. Two squadrons are reported to have scored as many as 122 kills during those days. Pilot Hans Student crashed in or near Arnhem on 26 September 1944. He was severely wounded and died a few days later in a hospital in Germany.

The forces Hitler made available also included all reserve ground units and units in training, present in *Wehrkreis VI* (Military district 6, Westphalia); as well as all troops in the Wesel area – altogether some 3,000 men – ready to cross the Rhine. Military district 6 was the original area of the 6th Army until its downfall in Stalingrad. The district bordered much of the Netherlands. New reserves were drafted here continuously as the war progressed. There also was a 2nd Parachute Corps, based in Cologne. Initially it was planned to have this corps attack the high ground of Groesbeek, but it had already been annihilated in Belgium.

Hitler also considered sending German army and navy units from Denmark, Central Germany and East-Germany to the Market Garden area. The numbers of military involved at that stage of the war and their qualities are not known but clearly, there were many thousands. Finally, this wide variety of haphazard counter measures is said to have caused Hitler to plan a large counter offensive. This resulted in the Ardennes Offensive, also called the Battle of the Bulge or just 'Bastogne', in December 1944. The Dutch called it the Rundstedt Offensive at the time which was maybe taken from BBC radio reports. Hitler's total forces grew to about 10 million in those months, by far the largest armed force of any country in history. These included poorly trained very young and very old men – invariably called *'das letzte Aufgebot'* (last reserves). Their combat capacities were below standard, of course.

As Hartenstein had become Urquhart's HQ, it was the starting point of what quickly became the perimeter of Oosterbeek, since the Germans succeeded quickly in breaking up the Airborne troops into three separate combat zones. Although 'perimeter' in itself is a mathematical concept only, it became emotionally charged with regards to Oosterbeek and the Battle of Arnhem. The Perimeter was a long and rather narrow zone in which the British and Poles were pressed together, roughly between the Hartenstein

As well as an incredible amount of debris in the street, a German 'StuG' tank and an Allied jeep are both on fire. British and German soldiers can be seen in the foreground. A German truck, of which the wrong window is shattered (continental drivers do not drive on the right) with a German driver hanging from the cabin's roof, is wrecked on *Bovenover* street. On the right, between the trees, is a street called *Onderlangs* (Underneath), which borders the Rhine. In the distance is Arnhem's icon, the Eusebius tower. The bridge is clearly visible, along with the smoke caused by the fighting between John Frost's men and the Germans. An orange glow of fire hangs over the city. Although the scene was painted in 1983, it is not an exaggeration of 1944's reality, as months after the war, many streets in Arnhem looked much the same. (*Rijnstate Hosptial*)

hotel, Roy Urquhart's HQ as long as it was, and down to the north bank of the Rhine. The size of the zone was about 1.6km (1 mile) long until the Rhine and about 200m (650ft) wide at first. The perimeter was where the British and Polish fought until they retreated. They were under nearly constant German fire.

The number of killed and wounded increased sharply during the final days. Homes in the nearby area including the Tafelberg were used as hospitals. One such house was the home of Mrs. Kate ter Horst. She lived next to the ten centuries old village church at the lower end of the Perimeter and took care of about 250 wounded and dying British paratroopers as performed by herself in the movie *Theirs is the Glory* of 1946 and by Norwegian actress Liv Ullmann in *A Bridge Too Far*. For this, Mrs. ter Horst was called the Angel of Arnhem by the wounded paratroopers. The British ambassador to the Netherlands decorated Mrs. ter Horst and her husband as Honorary Members of the Most Excellent Order of the British Empire in 1980.

If there was a turning point at all in the Battle of Arnhem, it was Tuesday, 19 September which had initially determined as the day for Arnhem to be relieved, in fact by 3pm. Instead, physical contact between the fighting zones was broken and could no longer be restored. German pressure increased while more units, tanks and heavy guns arrived. Meanwhile the weather was becoming very autumnal. It was raining and in the fields there was heavy ground fog in the early hours. It was hard for new supplies to be delivered. Conditions deteriorated rapidly for the British when, on Wednesday, there was still was no relief from XXX Army Corps. Besides, commander Urquhart had been missing for a few days. He was hiding in a private house next to Elisabeth's hospital after almost being spotted by some Germans. When he was free again, he did not know that Frost was on the bridge. Still he managed to return to his Hartenstein HQ.

Many Germans were wounded or lost their lives too, while over 450 civilians are believed to have been killed in the fighting in those days. Strange as it may seem, comparable figures for the number of civilians killed in the Nijmegen-Groesbeek area in 1944 could not be produced when asked for them late in 2015, over seventy-one years later, from the National Liberation Museum at Groesbeek. Isn't it another question at Nijmegen? It is clear that the defeat of the two Allied combat units in the Arnhem area, one British division and less than half a Polish brigade, was owed to a number of reasons beyond their control.

It was planned that the larger part of the Polish brigade, including one company, was to land near Driel, opposite the Rhine, three days later. But due to heavy German fire the transports turned away and dropped their men between Nijmegen and Grave. Unable to join their comrades at Driel, they stayed near Grave for two days, then marched to Nijmegen. At Oosterbeek and Arnhem all operations had ceased by then. Widely around Oosterbeek, an unknown number of troops roamed the forests. Among them there was one American pilot who had been downed and an unintelligible Russian.

Market Garden and the Battle of Arnhem were concluded in a rather exceptional way. Not in a regular press-meeting as so many were, let this be clear, as this cheerless end of Market Garden and the Battle of Arnhem was anything but a reason for a press conference. It was in a closed military meeting, a eyewitness account of which can be found as Sosabowski was involved. While XXX Corps was still in Nijmegen, its 43 Wessex Division had advanced to Valburg, a small town south of Driel. Its HQ was a large tent.

A conference of a few high ranking British officers, including Browning and Horrocks was held in this tent on 24 September. Sosabowski was told to be present. The meeting looked rather like a court-martial, with all the British officers on one side of a table and only Sosabowski on the other. Major General Thomas, speaking for Horrocks, announced that the following night two one-way crossings of the Rhine from the south were planned near Driel. They were to support the Airborne troops at Oosterbeek. Browning had no say in this discussion. It was a very strange announcement indeed since the fighting north of the Rhine had ended a few days earlier. In the end, the situation convinced Browning that there was no other choice but to evacuate the remaining airborne troops from the Perimeter. He reported this to Miles Dempsey, who agreed. The decision to withdraw was approved by Montgomery on the next day. He agreed, later, that serious mistakes had been made.

Three actions were deployed to relieve as many Airborne units as possible from Oosterbeek, the first one as suggested by Urquhart. They were all very dangerous because of the speed of the Rhine and its current, and many were drowned. The first rescue saved about 2,400 men. It took place in the night of 25/26 September from the lower end of the Perimeter. About 95 were killed, by drowning and by German fire from surrounding higher grounds. As the Dutch recalled, the Rhine was 'red with blood'. A monument is in place where the rescued entered the dike between Driel and the rail bridge. British, Polish, Canadian and Dutch flags wave while wreaths and flowers are laid at this monument each year.

The second relief operation was named Pegasus. It took place during the night of 22/23 October and involved a patrol of Easy Company of 506 PIR (the *Band of Brothers*). This operation took place some 5km (3 miles) west of the Perimeter, where today's A50 motorway bridge is located. Among the 139 men to be saved were British soldiers, a few American airmen, Russians and Dutchmen. There were Germans in the area who opened fire on them. No one was hit, but one Russian was arrested before entering a boat. The operation took only ninety minutes and was a success for all who crossed the river. A modest monument was raised to remind us of this rescue action.

Pegasus inspired someone in the Betuwe or Nijmegen area to become a reporter on the Dutch and Allied troops. His story about the action was read by the Germans, who now intensified their patrols along the Rhine to prevent more such relief actions and wipe out as many British as possible. As a result, Pegasus II became a bloody disaster. It took place during the night of 18/19 November. The plan was to bring 130 to 160 civilians, across the Rhine. But they were found by German patrols and in the end, only seven men managed to cross. Here, too, a monument is in place with the names of those who lost their lives in the rescue. Most of the British who were saved got home. That was the regrettable end of such a courageous operation of the British 1st Airborne Division and units of the 1st Independent Polish Airborne Brigade.

Sosabowski, however, was relieved of his command and dismissed by Polish president in exile Wladislaw Raczkiewicz in December 1944 which was totally unfair. Sosabowski stayed in Britain, working in a factory, until he was pensioned off. He died on 25 September,1967. The reputation of this man and his brigade was 'rehabilitated' by the Dutch government in the 1990s, even though no Dutch military men or officials were involved in Sosabowski's downfall as a military leader in 1944.

Chapter Sixteen

Railways on Strike

Day One of Market Garden was also the day when the Dutch government in London ordered a countrywide railway strike. The first and general aim was to hamper German transportation of all kinds. A second reason was to protect – in a rather peculiar way – passengers from more air attacks. The entire work force of Netherlands Railways (called NS), at least some 30,000 men and women, were involved and also included those of separate interurban rail companies. Unlike the rumours of early September, Market Garden looked like the real liberation this time. As NS was a state ruled company, the order was issued by the Dutch government in exile in London. The strike was proclaimed at 6pm by radio. The management in Utrecht just had to follow suit in this case, but there were some good reasons as well.

Since 1940, thousands who were in hiding from the Germans were given shelter by NS. Many were NS employees, Resistance workers, or even both, and all received new IDs issued by NS. But NS also contained Nazi-sympathizers. Following the strike, many could no longer be given shelter, as all kinds of structures, such as stations and shops were deserted, unheated and no longer staffed. The initial idea was that a strike was needed for only a few weeks during Market Garden, and probably during ensuing combats. But when Market Garden had failed, there were no longer revenues. 'Legal' railway employees and their families had to be paid monthly incomes somehow. This had been organized quickly in the first place to ensure such payments to relatives of seamen who had escaped since 1940, but it was quickly expanded on behalf of those in hiding with NS.

There had been appeals for railway strikes from London before, but they had been ignored. Besides, Germans had threatened to block all domestic food transports by train. Such strikes would damage their military transports to the Netherlands, they reasoned, as much as their different transports out of the country. Many train loads included the removal of substantial parts of the machinery from Philips in Eindhoven in 1944 and other manufacturers, to replace similar equipment bombed out in Germany or Czechoslovakia. Even worse, much worse, were the transports to bring Jewish citizens from several cities to Westerbork camp in the Netherlands and from there to the gas chamber death camps of the holocaust, like Auschwitz or Sobibor.

Railways on the continent were subjected to Allied attacks from the air, to damage German interests in the first place, albeit thousands of citizens in different countries suffered as well. In the Netherlands, Allied pilots carried out 435 special air strikes on locomotives, passenger and freight trains from 28 May 1944 until 17 September 1944. Most air strikes were carried out by the RAF, using Typhoons, Spitfires or Beaufighters. The highest number of single daylight attacks was thirty-nine on the afternoon of 5 September, which was also Mad Tuesday, coincidentally.

There were also RAF and USAAF Lockheed Lightnings in the air. They were of exceptional twin-boom tails design, like the Fokker G-1 bomber-fighters of 1936. The Lightnings or P-38s were much feared by German pilots because of their high speed, high degree of manoeuvrability and their merciless Oldsmobile- and Colt-made guns, which fired much larger bullets than used in aviation warfare before.

Air strikes hampered train schedules and delayed trains for hours, if not for the rest of the day or longer, depending on the damage done. These attacks had great impact on passengers and witnesses. They left long-standing memories, both on engineers, other employees and passengers. Even deep into the sixties, people used to tell each other often and relive shocking war-time experiences, almost every day somewhere. Those on train rides, being subjected to heavy shootings from the air, had about the greatest impact, as many experienced such attacks as personal assaults.

Much later, in the late seventies, I once joined an engineer in the cabin of an all-new type of electric train, from Amsterdam to Nijmegen, in view of a newspaper feature to be written on that type of train. Incidentally, at some place between Arnhem and Nijmegen, the engineer suddenly exclaimed: 'Here it was exactly!' Here was what? In the summer of 1944 the engineer was a steam engine stoker, as he explained:

'We hadn't been notified of any air activity prior to leaving Arnhem', he told me, 'as it was usual if there was a danger from the air. All of a sudden three RAF fighters swarmed over and around us. Next they disappeared for a few minutes while we tried to stop our passenger train at break-neck speed. Passengers were excited, full of fear and very nervous. They had seen the aircraft as well and were fully aware of what was ahead. They left the train from both sides of the coaches, as quickly as they were able to. They were nervous for fear of being hit and went to find cover opposite the ditches along the railway embankment.

'This was always very risky. For example, another train might still be coming towards us.'

Most coaches for inland rail traffic in those days had no corridors, but separate doors on each side of every compartment. The long running boards of steam era passenger coaches were hung over at least 1 metre over the maintenance footpath along the track.

'Meanwhile, the aircraft could come back at any moment, or even before we had come to a halt. And if any passengers were very young, old or handicapped, escape was even more dangerous. Many couldn't face the scary jump from the train. Others stumbled, many fell, injuring themselves in the jump, when tripping over the tracks or when running away, and even fell into the ditches on both sides of the embankment. Many risked taking cover underneath the trains!

'Finally, those of us manning the engine, had to take care of ourselves, as soon as we had stopped the train. In many cases, there were very small concrete shelters on the tenders for cover. If we had time, we helped passengers who were in trouble. We were not able to contact any emergency services ourselves. However, people in surrounding houses and farms usually did that for us if they could, but in those days most people had no telephone in their houses. Then, albeit often before everyone had been able to get away from the train safely, the shooting began.

'Although they aimed at the steam engine', the engineer continued while minding the signals and the crossings, 'bullets flew and hit us indiscriminately. Anyone, ourselves or passengers could be wounded or killed. Usually the aircraft pilots dived and attacked two or three times, then disappeared. In most cases they could judge pretty well if the engine was hit. In such cases, steam escaped from various sides. If it had been hit, we were stranded. If it hadn't been, we waited until "all clear" was announced, and then we had to make people board the train again. This, however, took more time than exiting the train, because of the height of the coaches. It was also complicated by trying to help those who had been wounded or killed; or because people had lost their nerves and wouldn't get back on the train. Delays were enormous. They were far from pleasant working conditions.'

At least 300 passengers and 200 NS employees were killed during the Allied shootings before 17 September 1944. There are no official casualty figures. The aim was to destroy steam engines. This was a useless effort, as there were sufficient numbers of steam engines to replace broken engines, while those that were broken were repaired quickly. Besides, Wehrmacht trains always came first. Not a single Allied purpose was served when electric passenger trains were fired at. Allied fighters attacked German freight trains after October 1944, which were believed or reported to carry V-1 flying bomb and V-2 rocket components from Germany to The Hague. In most cases, due to poor aiming equipment then, such air attacks proved fruitless. This included attacks of freight trains on rail bridges on the IJssel river between Arnhem and Zwolle and launch sites. Collateral damage and direct fire however has resulted in the killing of 1,044 civilians at least.

Small wonder that certain unpleasant visual or aural experiences of the war, and even special odours or tastes, have settled deep into the minds of many, any of which could be relived, suddenly, even many decades after, without any specific relevance at such moments. As late as 1948 or 1949, I remember seeing a large number of contrails one day, high in the skies, all in the same direction on a sunlit afternoon. As the war was over, what could be threatening about contrails. But suddenly the contrails were there and so there was fear again. Were they bombers? Maybe yes, but maybe they were a formation of RAF or USAAF bombers, on their way to whatever air force base in a defeated, occupied Germany.

In 1948, there had been peace for over three years and of course there was no ack-ack fire any longer. No noises to remind us of the war and no more fighters swarming around to attack. There was nothing to worry about, was there? But even after decades, the war could be a strong memory. The war and its horrors, *verschrikkingen* as the Dutch say, was still 10 per cent of one's life at an age of 50. All kinds of shock and fear dating back to those years might pop up once more after decades and cause another mental shock without a good reason.

As the failure of Market Garden had split the country into two parts, millions north of the rivers were deprived of quantities of daily food for the remainder of the occupation, regardless of the scarcity already existing. This has caused so-called *hongertochten*, individual hunger trips until the end of the war, to collect food elsewhere in the country. The railway strike also deprived people in the occupied area of coal from the south of Limburg for the winter, which was to become a very severe winter indeed. All domestic mail traffic stagnated as well. If people had to contact others outside their home towns, which included reports of relatives who had died or were ill, they depended upon friends and strangers to deliver a few letters if they were going somewhere. In most cases they were hunger trips. Consequently, many funerals could no longer be attended, since most telephone traffic

Destination sign for trains exclusively carrying Jewish citizens from Westerbork in the Netherlands to Auschwitz and back, which was recovered after the war.

was broken as well, entirely so between the liberated and the occupied Netherlands, families and other relationships were broken too.

As an example, Marius van Beek, who had escaped to relatives in Utrecht, was unable to inform his mother in Nijmegen of his whereabouts until the end of Market Garden. Only then did he manage to return to Nijmegen, crossing the front line secretly. All this, of course, added greatly to the country's social confusion to be deprived of so much, under continuing war time conditions. But it was nothing new for the Dutch cabinet members in London or NS management in Utrecht. Yet neither of these two most responsible parties announced a discontinuation of the railway strike and resumption of work to the railway men and women, when, only after a week, the failure of Market Garden had become clear. Such a resumption was badly needed, as the Germans now executed an earlier threat, a total obstruction of freight traffic as well.

Following this useless obstruction and total blockade of food, thousands of Dutch, women and youngsters under the age of sixteen mostly, had to leave their cities and try to buy food in the country, which produced yet another big social problem. Most had to travel on foot or their bikes, as petrol, tires and car parts were no longer available to citizens since the beginning of the war. But the Germans were not the only ones to blame for the lack of public transport; the Dutch government and the Board of NS were just as much to blame.

In fact, the Germans had far fewer problems with the strike, with an exception of the acts of sabotage in the next months. NS was absorbed by *Deutsche Reichsbahn*. Transports to be continued involved deportation of Jewish citizens to their killing camps in Germany and Poland. The very last rides of their lives. The transports also involved other Dutch citizens, as German convicts and round-ups for forced labour in Germany, including related products and capital goods manufactured by Dutch industries, were taken out of the country on behalf of German interests.

Finally, the Germans north of the rivers took a great deal of NS steam engines, many electric trains, all kinds of other freight and passenger rolling stock to Germany, just like in other occupied countries. Rail traffic south of the rivers, the liberated part of the country, was resumed, although means were limited. Much of the stolen stock was damaged in the next eight months, or remained in the Red sector in 1945, including Poland and some other countries. With the exception of what was found in Poland, most of this stock never returned and added to the NS total war damage.

Until the national railway-strike, the occupiers paid NS for transports in their interest. They may have been German prices, but they were still paid. In the case of transports of Jewish citizens until the railway strike, it was rather different. After the war it became clear that these transports were paid from yields of valuable private Jewish possessions, including gold from their teeth. It was a shock to the NS board when this came to light, when the war was over.

Chapter Seventeen

Eviction – Tramping like Vagabonds

The outcome of Market Garden was a deep disappointment to all concerned from the military standpoint as much as to the Dutch. South of the rivers, thirty-four Dutch towns and cities were taken from the Germans between 14 September and 3 December 1944. They included cities like Maastricht, Eindhoven, Nijmegen, Den Bosch, Breda, as well as several Luftwaffe bases. North of the rivers the Germans were despised even more. They knew it and the Dutch took pride in their own growing contempt. In turn, living conditions deteriorated once more, very seriously.

Hundreds of thousands of civilians could take advantage of the liberation in the southeast, although the war was all but over for those living there. They were freed human beings first of all and yes, there was a dear price. But you can't put a price on being free, which was particularly true for those who remembered the pre-war years. King George VI discussed living conditions when he visited the area in December 1944. He came as close to the frontline as Elst. He visited a family, who later had a crown carved into the simple chair he sat on.

There were still no German artillery in the street where I lived. But fear of what might be ahead in the case of a repulse, the kind of brute revenge the Germans might take, such as large-scale destruction of the city as they were known to do in the Soviet Union, was in the minds of many. Some people started to fear a German order to be expelled from the city for no specific reason. My parents, using sheets of paper on which they drew some sort of maps, tried to explain to me what was going on. Where, and what it was all about. What was 'here' and what was 'there', including several names and new words that I had heard a number of times over the last few days. Trying to explain as well that it was all about being free and being occupied. Leaving out, I guess, what might make their explanations somewhat complicated.

The difference between being free and being occupied was hard to explain and to understand, of course, for someone my age, just 5.

What might lie ahead was soon to arrive. One civil servant in Arnhem, Mr. G. van Helbergen, was taking care of totally bewildered refugees and wounded civilians who were hospitalized in a Catholic school. It was situated across from a local hospital that was overcrowded. The civilians had escaped from Arnhem, Oosterbeek and some other places. Van Helbergen was interrupted by a German orderly who arrived on a motor-bike. This was on Saturday morning, 23 September. The battle was just about over, but fear and bewilderment among those in the area remained. Many explosions could still be heard. Firing continued in the Betuwe, while the targets were downtown Arnhem. A city loved even by the Germans all during the war was now being used for some kind of target practice.

The population of the Arnhem area was still in shock, however, from what was perceived as an undeserved defeat of the good guys. And knowing the Germans well, a bleak defeat of our own hopes as well. Nearly everyone in the city and the country felt so sorry for the courageous British (while many Dutch were unaware of Polish involvement). They felt dismay, disappointment and sympathy. Germans behaved even more arrogantly than they had been doing since 1940 and they certainly were to be feared.

The orderly informed Mr. Van Helbergen that the entire population of Arnhem had to leave the city. And immediately, of course. But what could Van Helbergen do with this strange piece of information and why did the orderly talk to him in this school, this unusual place? Was he supposed to climb the spires of the city's towers and shout the latest news in four directions? An emergency hospital was equipped in the basement of the school, where Van Helbergen was busy helping people who needed all kinds of attention. He had other interests, even though it was all but his regular work. Permanent care had to be taken of wounded, of patients with different illnesses including contagious diseases, women in labour, dead to be buried. And now this; the city had to be evacuated.

Van Helbergen suggested the orderly talk to a Netherlands Red Cross official who was in the hospital across the street. There was total disorder among the city's government. The mayor, a collaborator, was at large. Van Helbergen believed that the Netherlands Red Cross, who had been busy since the earliest hours of 1940 in fact, was the best to organize an evacuation out of the blue on a scale like this. 'The city' involved a population of 97,000. They included elderly, hospital and rest home patients, physically ill or disabled, mentally ill, inmates in prison, ordinary men and women, children, newborn babies and their mothers. The school's basement was much needed, especially for people who needed mental health care all day. Many needed well-organized support when leaving the city.

Sometime in the afternoon, a few Netherlands Red Cross members, civil servants and Dr. W. Majoewsky from Amsterdam, as was reported after the war, met with a German orderly and some Wehrmacht officers. The Dutch were very busy in the hospital as well, just as Van Helbergen was in the school across the street, taking care of wounded and shell-shocked civilians. Following the recent fighting and the dangers they were exposed to, many were still very much distressed and confused. Chaos in the city, Oosterbeek and beyond was overwhelming.

Under these very hectic conditions, one civil servant listened with half an ear to a German orderly who garbled some sort of message. It was hardly noticed. The civil servant made it clear that he wanted a written confirmation in which it was also stated who – what authority – gave the order. A few others, among them a physician, explained later that one or two officers had entered the hospital and presented a written message. Clearly, there was turmoil all around. Dr. Majoewsky explained that 'a lieutenant or a captain' had told him: '*Die Stadt muss am Montag geraeumt sein. Mit Bombenteppichen muss gerechnet werden*'. 'The city must be evacuated on Monday. Carpet bombings are to be expected.'

The threat of carpet bombing was shocking – after Rotterdam in 1940 and four more years of large-scale, often horrendous German war crimes from Belfast to Belgrade and the Volga. Even so, the meaning of the message was such that it could not be accepted as an official order, to be carried out within forty-eight hours in a city where direct public information such as radio and newspapers were no longer available. Meanwhile, rumours and reports poured into the hospital. Some citizens did not hesitate and rushed out of Arnhem for Velp voluntarily on Saturday. Orders of evacuation were issued and spread throughout the city.

It seems the order to evacuate Arnhem, as well as neighbouring towns, was issued by an SS-general whose name was never found. He was a phantom. One Netherlands Red Cross manager, Mr. J.N. van der Does, was ordered to report at a spacious villa on the same afternoon, Saturday, 23 September at 4pm. The villa was on top of a hill near the provincial road to Deelen and Apeldoorn. It was supposed to be the general's military quarters, as well as his private house, like in Model's at Terborg. But it was HQ of the staff of the 9th Hohenstaufen Tank Division, while its commander, Bittrich, had moved to Doetinchem. Which implies that the legal Dutch owners of the villa had been ordered to leave, leaving behind all furniture for the use of the new occupant. At that time, there was no other SS general to be found in Arnhem.

Van der Does tried to obtain more information about what was wanted in the next few days and by whom. He acted in view of his responsibilities at the hospital, about a mile away, as the 'mayor' of Arnhem had left the city a few days earlier. Clearly, there was no authority in the city, neither from the civil side, nor the German. Van der Does was shown a note 'on behalf of the Divisional Command' with an illegible signature. The note was made out 'To the Commissariat in the Netherlands', whatever that might mean. Van der Does discussed matters with an SS-*Obersturmfüehrer*, a stupid, rude first lieutenant. The note read:

'As troop commander in the city of Arnheim, I have ordered the evacuation of the city of Arnheim for military reasons in the next periods:

'23.9.44: Evacuation of the southern districts [both sides of the Rhine] as far as the city tram line west to east.

'24.9.44: Continuation of evacuation in city centre district, between city tram and railway lines west to east.

'25.9.44: Evacuation of northern and remaining districts north of railway lines.

I draw attention to the fact that the entire civil population of the districts mentioned will have to have cleared [evacuated] the city without a right to return. Particulars will be given by the *Ortskommandantur* [city commander] and the *Hollaendische Raeumungsbehoerde* [Dutch evacuation authorities].'

Germany's military commander in Arnhem had been killed near Wolfheze on the 17th, while *Raeumungsbehoerde* was something of a false name. A municipal Office of Civil Deportation appeared to exist, but little was known about it and no one could be reached. In fact, nothing like this existed. The Netherlands Red Cross was the nearest from an organizational point of view. It was impossible to carry out this capricious order at such a short notice, given the hour of the day in the first place. It was the 23rd. It could not be checked either.

'For military reasons' was an unanswerable remark. Then they said: for fear of another Allied assault. But judicial examination or any other effort to have the evacuation order cancelled was entirely useless of course, even if it was made out by an SS first lieutenant. Once messages and orders were written down on a sheet of paper with a swastika, any messages were a law, not to be questioned. It was a strange order, as the residential district between the city tram line from west to east and the parallel railway is a rather narrow strip.

Yet, Van der Does immediately left the villa to obtain delay on behalf of patients and staff of the three remaining hospitals in use in town. He was given eight days on the spot – which looks like a confirmation of the capriciousness of the order – but the German added the previously heard threat: the carpet bombing of Arnhem. After an exchange of views with a few other Dutchmen, Van der Does decided to evacuate the three hospitals right away; there was to be no repeat of Rotterdam, 1940.

A few British wounded among the patients were told to be silent to everyone they did not recognize. Next to their uniforms, they were also stripped of their mother tongue for the time being, in order to survive. When ordered to present IDs, they were told to say *'verloren'*, lost. Meanwhile a man showed up at the hospital who claimed to be the new mayor of Arnhem. He, too, was known to be a collaborator. The Germans ordered the local fire department to circulate the order to leave all over the city instantly. 'Evacuate a city'. In those days it made no sense to question such an order.

People were ordered to leave their homes, homesteads and city, and this was not all. They – which is 'we' – were also ordered to go almost instantly and to leave behind almost everything from their homes. Small wonder if many were flabbergasted. Just a few pieces of clothing and some food was all we were allowed to take out, if we were lucky, some blankets and sheets. Lacking simple vehicles such as bikes, or other means of transport such as prams, small children's buggies, hand-carts or wheel barrows, people could only take essentials. We, the people, wondered what was ahead and where to go. Could we return within a few days? And if not, why not? But above all, what was this 'evacuation' all about? The question was raised by almost everyone. An evacuation is meant to be a temporary affair after all, to protect people and their belongings at the same time. Not a removal of unlimited duration, although it looked much like that.

Many in this rich-in-horses province, even today, owned large four wheel flatbed cars or coaches with which to carry people and many possessions. Trucks were used to carry hospital patients and the like. My father's bike was still his own. It was not stolen by Germans, maybe because an uneasy, dangerous wooden sort of 'tyres' had replaced the original rubber ones after they were worn out. Rubber bike tyres were available at black market prices only and they cost about 200 guilders a piece (£65, US$98 today). In those days, this amount, for one tyre only, equalled a factory worker's income for a month. Absurd. Meanwhile having one child only, they were lucky. But more needed to be carried by Arnhem's new refugees, more than just prime necessities. Clothes. Some convenient food for the next few days. Pets. Old, sick or disabled people. And what about families with many children? There were so very many large families in the Netherlands then, particularly among Catholic families.

My father's brother, Johan, his wife and their six-pack of youngsters were one of these, but what if you were forced in a position to make the herd survive under war time conditions? Fortunately, they possessed a pram, a buggy and two bikes, and at least three sons and a daughter were able to carry some items in bags or sacks for some time. However, an orphan, who had been adopted by the family after joining them as a domestic help, was also included and so clothes were needed for nine people. Most space in the buggy was taken by the youngest, who was 2 or 3 years old. A small pan was put on her head.

Buggies and prams could not be loaded too heavily, or wheels were sure to come off, axles broken. Many people were unaware of this and ran into trouble later. Clearly, almost anything else not needed in the first place had to be left behind. Furniture of course as much as cutlery, valuable paintings, beds, all those small and large belongings and anything else that make up an average household; private memories. Some people quickly dug holes in their yards or broke up wooden floors to cover their possessions. My father did so among his tobacco plants. But working men lost their jobs instantly, their business, their income, although other communities and municipalities were quick to organize systems to secure payments to those evicted. A few big companies like NS railways or ENKA of Arnhem acted similarly on behalf of their own staff. All kinds of food supplies throughout the city were lost – either through acts of war or to German robbery.

Leaving Arnhem. in this case towards Oosterbeek.

The summer, which had been a summer of hope for so many, was over. Thousands of young men, soldiers, had been killed in vain. People also lost their homes, as it appeared even more after the liberation. Until March 1945, no one had an idea when that liberation might be and how they would find their homes and property. All this while the weather was poor and misery was all over – mental and physical entanglement were in control of most people. Everyone was severely depressed because of the fate of the airborne troops. Were they all dead or taken prisoner? If there was a defeat, it involved the Dutch as well. Transport, meanwhile, was a mess. Where could people go? The eviction the Germans cruelly ordered in this area and their threat of carpet bombing, while we were vulnerable in the open, an eviction of which the criminal reasons became clear later, have all added strongly to the contempt many Dutch still feel when it comes to German inhumanity, especially among those with indelible war time memories of their own.

The first question was; where to go? Many had relatives in the area, or friends who could be reached for help and shelter for a few days. But it was a very short-lived prospect. Following the evacuation of Arnhem, citizens of a number of small towns to the west, Oosterbeek and Wolfheze as far as Wageningen, and to the southeast of Arnhem as far as the German border, were ordered the same; pick up a few things and leave. From Arnhem and beyond, at least 170,000 people were affected. There were many more, as people in the Betuwe and certain communities south of Nijmegen, such as Groesbeek, were evacuated as well. They were not forced by Germans in all cases, but rather because of continuing warfare in which so many houses were destroyed. These journeys were hard. For the men who pushed their laden bikes or carts. For little children as much as for the elderly. And what about pregnant women in their different stages of pregnancy? Many children were born along the roads then.

Those from south Arnhem took the Rhine bridge first which was still in place, then left Arnhem to the north, northeast or northwest. Those of battered Groesbeek were taken all the way to Flanders, Belgium, in early October. The number of different victims involved in the Nijmegen area is not known. The National Liberation Museum at Groesbeek has no figures of casualties related to the war, of any category. So many decades after the war, this is a real surprise. Against a back drop of a bridge too far, the prefix *National* sounds like a pretence too much in this case.

Increasing numbers of refugees from every district thronged Arnhem's main streets. Dozens in separate streets joined to hundreds and several thousands at the city's squares, pulling and pushing poor-looking bicycles and all kinds of carts with personal belongings, or just stumbled along on their own two feet. My parents and our neighbours, who were also relatives, after all, joined to form a group. Jackie Muusse and her elder sisters said 'Goodbye, house', and I joined them. My father pushed the bicycle which was loaded with what he could carry. We made a left turn down the street and we headed for Velp. At least our parents had a few more relatives or friends over there where we could stay, maybe for a few days or weeks. Our destination at Velp was not far. My father made some groaning remarks when we passed the mansion that had been confiscated, or rather, stolen, by Gestapo chief Hanns Rauter. The mansion looked deserted. Sentinels were no longer in place. This first evacuation trip was a rather short one. We were welcomed and we were safe.

Large numbers of refugees, tens of thousands of them every day, continued to leave Arnhem in three major directions; 20,000 to the northeast (Velp and beyond); 40,000 to the north (Apeldoorn and beyond); another 20,000 to the northwest (Ede); while the final 17,000 either spread across small towns of the Veluwe, or ignored the eviction order and secretly stayed at home. Their speeds were slow, especially up the slopes surrounding the city. After the heavy tensions of the past ten days and the sudden preparations to leave their homes and towns, many were exhausted even before they left. At the same time there was much German military supply traffic entering Arnhem from several directions. Meanwhile, the Germans did not drive the refugees out, nor were there any examples of revengeful actions, or carpet bombings of the city. But there was a lot of air activity which caused people to hide.

Those who were late in leaving Arnhem also became the first to notice large-scale burglaries in town. Shops and storage depots were the first targets of burglars. Private houses came next. Germans were the first to start organized burglaries, as Arnhem photographers revealed. A few photographers and others with cameras had stayed behind secretly. Unscrupulous Dutch robbers were next to strike. They included local citizens who had found shelter very nearby, just outside the inhabited districts, such as the houses and farms in the city's Open Air Museum. This enabled them to return to Arnhem to recover various items of their own, but also for robberies after dark. Food was scarce and was wanted most of course, for private consumption and for the black market, but anything else might be welcome, too, and was stolen with as much greed. Arnhem was all but entirely cleared. The city became some sort of ghost town.

A government-appointed commission has assessed the size and value of private damage to civilians of Arnhem in the summer of 1945. The damage affected about 40,000 families. In today's money, the amount of property destroyed and stolen amounted to £14 million or US$ 2.1 billion.

The Germans, seeing this, then ordered every man or woman to leave the city or risk the death penalty, a threat that had been in force – and acted

Germans loading privately owned trucks in the Arnhem Hoogkamp district. This photograph was taken secretly, in early 1945. Today, a copy of the photograph hangs from the looted house visible here, with the open front door.

upon – since 5 September, Mad Tuesday, not on behalf of the original owners, but in their own interests. Streets became deserted as days and weeks progressed, although it was very risky to be spotted by Germans or collaborators. Arnhem was clearly turning into everybody's casualty of war, not only for the Germans. The same was to be true for Oosterbeek and other towns in the area alongside the Rhine.

As a small family, my parents had found shelter at Velp, but not for long. Uncle Carel, who lived there as well, was much involved in local charity during the war. Now, he was in a position to materialize this at his own home and so he did, without taking a second breath. My father joined his brother's art of bread baking. He was badly needed in view of the sudden increased population. At the same time, they stopped their father from returning to baking. The elderly couple was supposed to sit down and relax – after having 'shaken hands with the English' downtown. Carel also offered shelter to his elder brother Johan and his family, as there was sufficient space in his house to take nine more people. The house now became inhabited by twenty-three within a couple of days, as a few more also made an appeal to him. He did not refuse.

Carel certainly was not the only person in Velp to offer shelter to relatives or friends from Arnhem. So, Velp became overcrowded. But the community of Rheden, of which Velp is the southwesternmost member, indicated that it was running into food shortages. Really? Without an eviction, even more quantities of food were taken to Arnhem every day before 17 September. So why did Rheden and Velp suddenly run into food shortages? A second reason was fear of casualties, since warfare continued very nearby. This of course was a very valid reason. Grenades exploded repeatedly. Air fights continued. Several people were killed when a V-1 flying bomb struck near Uncle Carel's house.

One grenade almost hit Carel himself as Plien recalls, his eldest daughter. While at work in his bakery in early October and disregarding a shelling barrage, which in fact lasted for two days, he just stepped forward when a grenade came through a window. It narrowly missed him and exploded loudly a few metres further on. A machine was torn up from its foundations. Carel himself was blown away from where he stood, badly knocked about, and was deafened for some time and very frightened for even longer. Windows shattered in his bakery, his nearby home and a large glass roof in between. It was a shambles; pieces of rubble, flew all around. His relatives, who were all in the basement because of the continuous firing, were shocked by the nearby explosion, but nobody was hurt, except Carel himself! The bakery had to be thoroughly cleared of rubble and pieces of glass. It could not be used for the next two days.

It appeared that the grenade was British, aimed at German Tiger tanks parked in a nearby street. Their presence had been reported by the Resistance. They were no longer needed at the front, but remained in the area as the Germans believed the Allies, the 2nd Army particularly, would strike again. Incidents like these, the V-1 bomb included, meanwhile convinced Rheden's municipality that it was far too dangerous to have so many people at Velp, locals, as well as refugees from Arnhem and other places in the area. All those from Arnhem at Velp then were told to leave again, but this time by the mayor of Rheden. It was not an eviction to make victims this time, but to save lives. So, we had to go once more.

Which way? My parents considered Breukelen in the west of the country, beyond Utrecht city, as it was there where my other grandparents lived. This was a distance of about 90km (54 miles) at least, to be covered on foot by people who certainly were not in a very healthy and relaxed condition. What distance would they be able to cover in one day? What kind of dangers could they expect to be exposed to? What route to take, as the shortest was right through the area where fighting and the airborne landings had taken place? Where and with whom might they be spending the next night?

Nevertheless, all personal items were packed and loaded again and we left, shortly after the order to go. The route was Schelmseweg, the road that leads in a big arc around Arnhem. It was the same route Dobie's 1st Battalion, comprising of around 700 men, had intended to take, to branch off and encircle Arnhem after landing, about two weeks earlier, but in the other direction. It was cold and raining when we left Velp, uphill around Arnhem. My clothes were not really fit for this type of weather. My parents felt like going to Ede on this day. They were refugees again. Myself included. In those days I have never had the idea of being a refugee. Being a child, I simply had to stay with my parents. Meanwhile we were all but the only ones. We were three in a very long row of people in similar conditions, Arnhemers as well. We entered Schelmseweg. At times I was allowed an uneasy seat on the frame of my father's bike. When sitting there became painful in my upper legs, I was to go on my own feet.

Meanwhile it was hard labour, as my father put it, having to push his heavily loaded, easily out of balance, jumping bike up the moraines. They're not so high but they are steep and the packed bicycle was hard to handle. After a few kilometres there was a real surprise. Over 95 per cent of Schelmseweg was surrounded by dense forest. Out of this, suddenly three men emerged. Two were German soldiers. The other one was a British soldier. He was the first paratrooper I saw. In his unfamiliar uniform and still wearing his helmet, he was much different from the contemptuous cooking pans of the Germans. He was a sight to behold. The man was a surprise anyway, being found near Velp, at the far other end of Arnhem as seen from the dropping zones. The British soldier may have found some sort of shelter for over a week, but how come the Germans managed to find him? Who had spotted him? Was there someone who betrayed his presence?

These questions remain unanswered. But several other Airborne troops, including officers who did not escape from Oosterbeek across the Rhine in one of the three relief actions (Pegasus I and II, Berlin) when Market Garden was over, managed to escape from German captivity with the help of Dutch civilians. Unless these British and Poles were sheltered for the remaining duration of the war, they were assisted by the Dutch Underground to escape south across the rivers and rejoin their forces.

It took great attention among many refugees, when the Germans emerged from the bush, their rifles pointed at their prey. It appeared that most people were seeing a British soldier for the first time. Some among the Dutch then started to shout, telling the captured man to keep courage in short or long phrases. At first sight, this looked like the expression of a somewhat surprising habit in this part of the Netherlands, to interfere with someone else's matters just like that, without being invited. It may happen everywhere among people in the Netherlands who are not at all familiar with each other, from inside a shop to a railway platform. Generally with good, social intentions, but why? In this case it may have caused some relief to the British POW, assuring him that he was not alone.

Others shouted bad names, aimed at the Germans. My father may have joined in with this. I do not remember what was said, but they definitely were not expressions in favour of the Germans or their super hero in the east. My mother interrupted my father which may be why I remember the incident so clearly. 'You'd better be quiet,' she suddenly said, 'or the Germans might shoot you!' There were no German comments which was another surprise. They took their prisoner in the opposite direction. Let us hope he survived.

There was a Netherlands Red Cross first aid post. Either at the city's zoo, or at least at the crossroads. People were offered cups of ersatz coffee, or something hot at least, which was needed in the poor weather. At the crossroads we entered the Amsterdam Road, or the northwestern artery from Arnhem to Ede, Utrecht and beyond. Part of it was dubbed Leopard Route on 17 September and it was at these crossroads, at the outskirts of Arnhem, where Dobie's 1st Battalion had intended to turn left on that day, to encircle Arnhem.

Travelling west from there, the area quickly became very different. After another kilometre or so, we passed a rural state called Lichtenbeek. There, we were surrounded by various military litter, a helmet, German gas mask drums, small leather ammo bags. People left the special bicycle tracks which run parallel to the main road, to avoid nasty surprises, such as visible and hidden hand grenades or booby traps. They were not really all over the place. But people warned each other, they were there.

There clearly were remnants of the recent fierce fighting here. There were large and small pieces, twisted and broken. Sharp explosives like grenades or mines might be among them. People had to watch their steps very carefully. People in uniforms with helmets on, some painted white, were pointing at particularly dangerous places, such as pot holes in the road. At the same time, there were certain wafts of unusual bad smells, wherever they came from. We continued our journey and it grew worrisome. The bad smells became somewhat more frequent as we continued. Then we passed a number of white, wooden crosses. On them, '1st Airborne Division' was painted or written vertically, 'Unknown British Soldier' on the horizontal cross beams. It shocked people and all of a sudden it was clear that the bad smell all around was from still unrecovered bodies. Many of them, British and Germans alike by the way, were not taken care of until the spring of 1945. Poor guys.

It was also noticed by the Muusse family on one of these days. They were going from Velp to Ede at first. Was it the closest we all came to the actual fighting just over a week ago? It is unquestionable, although, north of the Rhine, fighting the German superior numbers took place in three more areas. In the streets, many had seen almost every form of fighting in one way or another. Including soldiers screaming, or being knocked down for good. Far more than the noisy 'shambles' they caused, these last seconds were the worst part of it all. Eye-witnesses were to be found in Arnhem as much as in Oosterbeek and beyond. The perilous litter around on our way to Ede continued for several kilometres, while we travelled in a twilight of autumn cloudiness and dark forest, the wooded area between Arnhem and Ginkel Heath. This was where it all had begun as far as Operation Market Garden was concerned. The battlefield had turned into a battered area.

In the area from Arnhem to Wageningen, war continued after the brief pause in which the population left their homes. First, as soon as Frost and his men had given up, German tanks and other armoured vehicles crossed the Rhine bridge to counterattack the British. There had been lengthy fights in the area between Arnhem and Nijmegen. Then, on 7 October 1944, the bridge was bombed and destroyed by USAAF B-26 Marauders. This bombing had terrible material results.

The Eusebius tower was the city's icon. Fire had broken out during the Battle of Arnhem, but when we returned, most of the city's centre was flat, destroyed, while the proud tower was damaged for over three-quarters of its height. Tons of rubble coming down had destroyed much of the church, my grandfather's bakery and indeed the whole residential area. No one seems to have seen exactly what made so much of the Eusebius tower come down. It is presumed and accepted that the tower gave way to air pressure when the nearby Rhine bridge was bombed. During a heavy storm in July 1945, when more people had returned from eviction, most of the remaining towers remnants also came down. Again, no-one was hurt. The tower and church in the heart of Arnhem were restored, long after the war. As a token of restored peace and city pride, the highly symbolic tower now stands 8 metres taller than before!

Chapter Eighteen

Sheltered with Strangers

We arrived at the small town of Ede late in the afternoon. Continuing our slow journey as far as Breukelen on the same day was out of the question. My parents and I were cold, wet, tired and hungry. It was dark and our mobility was very poor. There were no relatives at Ede or anyone who expected to see us. We had to beg for shelter somewhere, just like hundreds of thousands of others from the Arnhem area in those days. It seems that my parents were unaware of the Netherlands Red Cross, who were also present at Ede to help refugees.

A niece of my mother, who lived in Haarlem actually – another 100km (62 miles) – was engaged to marry someone at Ede, who lived at his parents' house. Their marriage had been postponed as a result of the war – it was hard to find a place to live. Living in the same house before being married, 'like husband and wife' as people called it, was not done then. The groom-to-be was a young school master who knew a lot of people. Maybe he could be of some help to us. We went there and rang at the door. The young man knew my mother and yes, he knew very well about the fate of Arnhem's population.

Actually, his parents had offered shelter to a young couple a few weeks earlier. They happened to be one of my mother's brothers and his wife, who was a sister of this school master, and who also lived in Arnhem. They had married on the last day of August and coincidentally, the couple had been forced to stay with her parents since 17 September. The couple had intended to pay a social visit to her parents on that sunny Sunday. They had passed Ginkel Heath on their bicycles, maybe an hour before the first parachutists came down. Obviously, they had not been able to return to Arnhem.

Yet we were welcomed as well: 'Just come in'. A meal was prepared for the shivering trio and make-shift shelter was offered for the night. But it was warm and it felt so comfortable there. Unfortunately, this could not be for long, as the events that had taken place in Arnhem had affected the other couple as well. In other words, the eviction by the Germans also involved people in other towns and hit or even damaged their privacy in a most serious way. Because of the curfew, no one was allowed outside until the next day.

A somewhat complicated solution was found on the next day. Following mediation by the Red Cross or Ede's municipality, a clergyman was prepared to have the three of us in his house temporarily during the day, for a limited number of days or weeks, while meals were offered to me only. The three of us could not sleep in his house, although it was a very large house, since he had also given shelter to other refugees from the Arnhem area. To solve this, it was decided we would spend the day with the clergymen at Ede, but the nights at the house of the man who was not a relative yet, while the recently married couple decided to go and stay with other relatives in Gouda for the time being. Meanwhile, my parents were to see if we could continue to my grandparents at Breukelen and stay there – if room allowed – for who knows how long.

And this was not even all. Netherlands Railways were on strike with no trains or intercity buses to Gouda or Breukelen and no intercity post traffic. Besides, long distance telephone calls had been paralyzed by 'the occupier' since 17 September or just after. So, how to reach all relatives concerned, how much time would be involved while waiting for answers and where to go if answers were negative? To start with, my father wrote a letter to his parents-in-law, my *other* grandparents. Being in town on the same day, it was helpful when he met with someone from Arnhem he knew. This man was to travel to Amsterdam. He took the letter with him, this third request for shelter in fact, and delivered it at Breukelen on the next day.

People were very helpful in those months. Even over a year after the war was over, people reached out to those from Arnhem and beyond. Textile and clothes came from as far away as a school in Berkely, California. Our stay for an unspecified period of time was not a very pleasant one and we were not the only ones to experience this. Both parties involved, refugees who had lost income as well as those who gave shelter, were paid allowances and were given additional rationing coupons by town councils. But refugees had little or nothing to do and stayed at the homes of those who gave shelter, rather than running a risk of being 'caught' by the Germans. Conditions were such that every man of about 18 to 45 years old was sure to be apprehended as soon as he left his home. There were no German man-hunts every day, but no one knew when and where the next raid was to take place.

Our sudden presence was an invasion of the privacy of the clergyman's family. It caused tensions between the clergyman and his family members. To avoid all this, my parents spent the evenings with their relatives-to-be. In the course of every evening they left the house to wake me up, as I had been asleep in the clergyman's house. They ignored the curfew, awoke me, dressed and rolled me into a blanket, to protect me from the cold. Then they took me into the open, to bring me to the other house and sleep there for the rest of the night. I was told not to make any noises while we went from one house to the other, as patrolling Germans shot at everything they believed suspicious and also, an unknown number of Red Devils and Poles were still at large.

Being in the street in daylight became even more dangerous for Dutchmen up to 45 years old, when the Germans decided to take more of them to carry out defence work, either in the area or in Germany. Well aware that Ede was crowded by refugees, they took whoever they preferred. Early in November the Germans decided to extend these round-ups to people's private houses. They called it *huiszoeking*, house search, one of those many linguistic barbarisms adapted from German (*Haussuchung*) which entered the Dutch language during the war. It was comparable to Apartheid, which the Dutch understand very well. Unannounced *Haussuchung* was an age old German habit, but it was unfamiliar to the Dutch. In brutal Nazi-style, they rang or knocked at the door and just entered, to look around for men. If found, they were taken to one of several barracks at Ede. This also occurred one day to the man, the school master whose name was Karel, who had invited us to come in. My parents and I were not there when it happened.

As a matter of fact, Karel had taken some precaution in the case of house search. He had turned his parent's long sofa into a shelter, into which he could hide very, very quickly, in case Germans showed up in the frightening and brutal way they used, such as hitting the door with the butts of their rifles, screaming '*Aufmachen!*' loudly (Open up). And so it happened on one day. The Germans, an officer and two men, searched the house, as they were sure men lived here. That is, the soldiers went through the house thoroughly, while the officer sat on the sofa. He noticed nothing of the man stretched out just below him, who for sheer nerves was almost trembling. But having found no-one, the three Germans left, much to the relief of all who were in the house, including Karel, who stepped out of the sofa.

'That was close!' everybody sighed, but then the officer again rang at the door. Again: '*Aufmachen!*' He had left behind his gloves, he said, pushed aside the one who had opened the door and went to the living room immediately; front doors and living room usually are separated by a corridor in the Netherlands. No time was left for Karel to open up the sofa again and jump into, so he flashed under the sofa. It is true that the German had left his gloves on the sofa. He took them, then looked around emphatically and left. This time 'that was close' even more and Karel took some extra time before appearing again. Actually, no one in the house believed that the German had left his gloves in error.

A letter arrived from my grandmother at Breukelen a few days later, early in November. Having been unable to find us during the Battle of Arnhem, while fearing the worst in our case, only now could she report that her husband, my other grandfather, had died on 19 October at the age of 79. It was very sad news. Being unaware at the time, my parents had not even been able to attend the funeral. At the same time, my grandmother suggested my parents to come to Breukelen. Her house, where she now lived with her youngest daughter only, was big enough to have three more people. So, once again, our personal belongings were packed. And again, it was a cold and raining day when we left Ede to make for Breukelen. The journey took a whole dreary day once more. We felt like tramps.

Just before entering Breukelen, we were alarmed by the very unpleasant approach of a V-1. They were called buzz bombs or doodlebugs in Britain. This very noisy flying bomb as it was also called, a forerunner of today's cruise missiles, was most probably aimed at Antwerp, fired from the northern province of Friesland. The V-1 was a most fearful weapon, as it was rather unreliable. The pulsejet engine could stop suddenly while it carried a warhead of 850 kilos (1,870lb). About 30,000 were built, most of which were fired from the Netherlands. In total, 9,521 were fired at Britain and another 2,448 at Antwerp. As for us, we hastily took shelter under some trees, which was a ridiculous precaution, of course. The V-1 roared by.

About a quarter of an hour later, in the dark and while it was raining yet again, we arrived at my grandmother's. It was our accommodation for the rest of the war. One of my father's first steps was to find a place where he could make a very hard-to-find shelter to hide, in a case of *'Aufmachen!'* I was never told where this hiding place might be. I only remember a few times when he rushed upstairs, but it was not because of Germans. We stayed with my grandmother until early August 1945, in fact, three months after Germany's downfall. This was during the worst part of the war in which the pig food was prepared.

While our own journeys from Velp to Ede and to Breukelen later were far from holiday trips, leaving Velp was a lot more challenging for my father's brother, Johan Kuiper. They also had to leave Velp behind. But where to go? His brother Carel, the one with the grenade entering behind his back, first suggested his brother stay in Velp, because of the size of his family. But Johan believed this was not fair really in respect of so many others. Carel then managed to find an open carrier tricycle to carry the clothes, blankets and some household freight of his brother's family, a most welcome means of transport, next to the two bicycles and the pram with which they had left Arnhem. But with the number of small children and in fact no idea where to go, uncle Johan's family of nine persons including himself (and the orphan), while the oldest child was only twelve, faced a real challenge. It took them most of a day in poor, autumn-daylight and rain to cover about 16km (10 miles). 'We all were cold and dead tired,' his second son John remembers.

Fortunately, they had bread, cold hotpot and a few knives and spoons with them, to have a meal at the road-side. Father Johan took a few notes of this meal for his diary. His eldest daughter Caroline recalls that the slices of bread were 'pure', as there was no butter or anything else. The idea was to head for Groningen province in the north, where they had lived until the outbreak of the war.

'But Groningen is 170km (102 miles) from Arnhem. How many days would it take to get there? Then, after16 km, we were stopped by a constable who directed us to Otterlo, a hamlet in the woods and another 15km.'

Her younger brother Paul adds:

'We all cried a lot in those terrible days. Mummy, we are so tired. And of course: is this Otterlo? Every time when we passed a curve and faced still another stretch of road. At one moment, our father put us all on the carrier and pushed the whole thing, together with our mother. But it was an uneasy ride. The road was unpaved. It was a sand road with many pot-holes, puddles and mud. It was such a silly experience.'

Then there was one peasant who distributed apples to the refugees. 'Here', he said, 'take them for your own, rather than having to wait until the Germans will pinch them.' For decades, it is one of those thousands of very small memories that have survived the worst part of the war. Once at Otterlo, they were approached by a local constable. He tried to think of some place for the night, when his wife arrived. She knew where to go. 'Come on,' she said, 'all of you.' She took the whole exhausted family inside and offered a meal, cleaning facilities and shelter for the night. The next day, Johan and his herd left for the village of Barneveld. There, they sent a message to still another family member, our grandad's brother, Hein, in Baarn. He also owned a large house and he also was the owner of a bakery. Great-uncle Hein urged Johan's whole family to stay at his house for the rest of the war.

Baarn was more or less at the edge of the area where hunger prevailed in the months to come. In spite of this, Hein made room in his home for a few others who were evicted from Arnhem as well. They included Jackie's family, my little friend next door. Today, over a 100 years after being established, Hein Kuiper's bakery in Baarn is still in business. Hein's great-grandson Sylvester owns it and executes the art of bread baking now. Like countless other experiences including our own – my parents and me – they are as much exemplary of those in the dreary autumn and very bad winter of 1944–45. Only those who had decided to go to the north east, or Friesland in the north sooner or later, did not suffer from food shortages and hunger. Many thousands from the Arnhem area were given lodging or shelter for unspecified periods by 'strangers' elsewhere in the country, in most cases as long as the country was occupied.

After Market Garden, scarcity of food and physical terror increased and living conditions became much worse in the occupied northern half of the country. The 1944–45 winter became severe in late November, with more snow in December and this added to this misery. The paper shoes I wore when leaving Arnhem wore out and had to be replaced by *klompen*, wooden shoes. They were new to me and anything but comfortable. They were small and hard to wear, they slipped from my feet in the snow (I also slipped in the snow), and caused painful blisters. Plus, they were cold, even when itchy straw was added. Finally, they were noisy as if I was a peasant's son. It was another war-time experience which I did not like at all. However – did the cold at home and in the street, poor clothing, inferior food and daily hunger affect my parents, grandmother or me? The cold, fear of Germans, fear of bombings and air fights all certainly did. But I do not have any recollection of diseases during those dreary months.

The Germans started systematic public round-ups of men aged 18 to 40 – this was as well as their pouncing on men in the street and taking them off to Germany as forced labour. These new round-ups were called *razzias*, and could be traps set up in streets or outside built-up areas. Sometimes the Germans went from house to house as they did at Ede. The first of these *razzias* was on 15 September. It was followed by round-ups in several townships. The word was not Dutch, but it quickly spread over the country and for obvious reasons it was widely feared.

On the same day, it was announced that there would be a further reduction in the supply of coal and gas across the country. The reason given was to save on coal. It was a half-truth. The real reason was that coal mined in the Netherlands was taken to Germany for use in their industries and households. Coal gas had restricted to three periods each day and would now be restricted to one period each day between 5pm and 7.30pm only, from 22 September.

The scope of man-hunts and scarcity were increased on 17 September. Next to men, more bicycles were also wanted. 'Wanted' means that they simply took them at random from Dutch owners, not just when they were parked, and sometimes they ordered riders off their bicycles whilst they were actually on them. Bikes were about the last means of transport that could be taken from the Dutch. This callousness earned the Germans yet another nickname for decades to come, *fietsendieven* (bicycle thieves). On the same day, there were further restrictions on the use of telephone lines and telegraph lines were completely terminated.

The Germans forbade all food supplies from other parts of the country to the West in late September and soon supplies hit a catastrophic low. Most towns had food stored in warehouses but it quickly ran out, especially as there were no imports or domestic supplies. A ban on food transports of 'any large quantities' to the west of the country in barges was imposed in late November. This deprived hundreds of thousands of families from major supplies of food, as well as peat and coal for heat. Potatoes, sugar, carrots and vegetables are grown in the west of the country, but much of that stock had been sent to Germany since 1940. Grains are not grown in the west, though needed by all families.

It was the Germans' revenge – but for what? Because of the incredible enthusiasm with which the Allies were supported? That is seen as the most probable reason. Meanwhile, the shortages and hunger increased rapidly. Then, realising that the downfall of Hitler's regime was imminent, Germans in the Netherlands started to destroy the port buildings and quays in Amsterdam and Rotterdam on 21 September, right in the middle of Market Garden. Shortly after, when the national railway strike was in force, the Germans started to take down overhead copper wires, and to lift rails unless they needed them for their own trains or for stealing locomotives, coaches and freight cars. They did this in other occupied countries too.

More rationing and food shortages were introduced on 1 October and again in late November. Availability of potatoes for example was reduced from 3kg to 1kg per week. For very many, this was about the only vegetable they had been able to buy, since most others had disappeared long ago. Sugar supplies were terminated in late October, just as the beets were harvested. City gas supplies to Amsterdam, Rotterdam and The Hague were terminated entirely in October and November, just when it was getting cold. Systematically or when considered appropriate, the Germans limited whatever they could, including water from the tap. City trams disappeared and services were ended around this time too.

The power shortages hit several neighbouring communities, meaning millions of people were affected, just as those in the Arnhem area had been after the bombing of 22 February 1944. It became very clear that 'Going West' had been the wrong choice for Arnhemers in view of the ongoing restrictions of food supplies, the severe war conditions of Market Garden and the ensuing eviction of other Dutch citizens. But since newspapers and other sources of news had been virtually banned, relatively few people were aware that serious, wide-spread famine was a fast approaching prospect for those in the west of the country.

The average daily bread consumption in the Netherlands can be compared to that of the Britain or America. Bread was limited to 800g (28.2oz) each, per week between mid–November and mid–December 1944. As a matter of fact, the Germans ordered even smaller rations, but as a result of Red Cross interventions and flour imported from Sweden, the levels were maintained or even increased sometimes. But what kind of bread were we talking about? A so-called 'government bread' was introduced in 1940. It contained limited quantities of grain flour per kilo, plus potato flour and ground dried peas and beans. People did not like this 'government bread' at all, since it was kind of spongy and somewhat sour, a flavour most Dutch do not appreciate at all. But there was no choice. It was available until 1960, albeit the ingredients and taste were much better after 1945. Government bread was considered 'poor man's bread' then.

Naturally, the government's bread production affected the availability of beans for other uses, including those to be used to replace meat products which they are good for, though with a different taste. So replacements for beans in bread had to be found when they run out as well. A very *natural* product was found, albeit a most unusual one. It was sawdust. After the mixed dough had become baked bread in the oven, the taste was not all that different from bread without sawdust, as long as the sawdust did not catch fire! But once more, what kind of bread are we talking about? What we could get was better than nothing at all.

Supplies of all groceries, butter, margarine and vegetable oil were terminated by late November, while double skimmed milk supplies were limited to youngsters under thirteen only. This was not only due to Germans, who took most of the milk for Germany. Many farmers refused to sell milk to the plants, because they were forced to supply the Germans. Milk was washed away into their ditches – and thus no longer for sale to civilians either. All these, and other steps to limit or even terminate availability and starve as many Dutch as possible applied to the west of the Netherlands only.

A 1945 sketch of a '*centrale kuken*', a Dutch soup kitchen. The blackboard explains which rationing coupons are required for which quantity of soup. In this case, coupon 369 is for potatoes, 371 for sugar carrots and 373 for beans. Double or triple standard portions were supplied against double or triple coupons and cash only. Fortunately, no separate coupons were needed for water, heating, or entering and leaving the soup kitchens. Breathing was also free.

It should be added that today's supermarkets, where all kinds of food are available, did not exist in the Netherlands back then. For groceries, one applied to the grocer; for milk, eggs, cheese and butter to the milkman and so on. They were all separate shops, separate owners, sometimes in different streets, in fact like in any European country in those days. Shopping might take several hours, even more when shop-keepers had to tell their clients that goods were not available a hundred times a day. The worst time came in December. Jam and salt were the very last groceries taken from us. This, depriving the Dutch of jam and salt, certainly was believed – in German minds – to be a major step to restrain the Allied tanks and forces from further advances towards Germany.

People suffered severely from the immense food shortages, even though virtually every community and city took care of public soup kitchens, where every day some kind of soup was supplied. The 'soups' were made from potatoes, sugar carrots, beans, stuff like that and, of course, mostly, water. Certain limited quantities of soup were supplied in exchange for money and rationing coupons. The taste of the soup, although prepared with the best of intentions, was like flavoured water. The experience of these terrible soups lingers on even today. When the Dutch say 'this is not much of a soup' (*niet veel soeps*), they mean something is inferior. Thousands got sick. After a time, very many people suffered from oedema. Some people died in the streets, just as they had in Amsterdam. Citizens of The Hague, Leiden and Haarlem areas turned to tulip bulbs for sustenance, which they fried in salad oil. It was most disgusting, one friend told me later, when he fried tulip bulbs again 'to recall the taste of the war'.

Those living in any size of community in the West turned to rural areas and farmers to obtain milk or food of any kind. It was one way to by-pass the shortages in food and fuel imposed on us. Often, we bartered all kinds of articles for food – fur coats, jewellery, silverware or valuable paintings. As a result, prices rose sky-high for those who had nothing to trade with. A small packet of margarine, 250g (8.8oz) went up from 40 cents to 140–160 guilders in early 1945. It was a pleasant sensation in my grandmother's house when one of us had managed to obtain a sugar carrot by Christmas. At the same time more and more farmers got fed up with all that was offered to them. Many were rather wealthy when the war was over – and had earned a very bad name among other citizens until long after the war.

Once or twice a week, my parents left Breukelen at about six in the morning in the freezing cold, to obtain some milk. Many farmers refused to sell as they did not know my parents. Sometimes it was helpful when my mother mentioned her father's profession as a publisher. He also sold Bibles, and he had also been the organist in Breukelen's small protestant church, hadn't he? 'Ah, yes, I knew him,' some farmers would say and then, some fresh, unskimmed milk was made available, which at home was churned, to prepare some butter first and to prevent all of us from getting sick from the high level of fat. Because by sheer luck, the smart Germans had fallen short of rationing grass in the summer of 1944.

But this didn't work in all cases. Several times my parents came home 'empty handed' as they put it. In those days, porridge cooked with rye, which was pig food, was our standard meal. A young cousin of my mother, Piet Buizer, ventured to the east of the country to try and obtain some food or raw vegetables for us to eat. He was gone for several days or even weeks. Thousands of others from the West made similar journeys. And like them, Piet had to walk whilst pushing his bike, because the bikes lacked tyres. People called these tough and dangerous trips 'hunger journeys' (*hongertochten*).

Such trips were by no means free from risk. People returning might be robbed by other Dutchmen or individual German soldiers, particularly when they had managed to obtain meat, sausages or vegetables. My mother experienced it herself when she made a hunger journey to the eastern town of Aalten, way beyond Arnhem. She went there in January and she returned at least two weeks later, as she had to walk all the way. Dad was unable to join her, as he would have been captured and forced to do labour in Germany. When mum returned, about half of the food she had managed to source had been acquired by others. For example she had to pay a ferryman for rowing her across the wide and fast streaming IJssel river with food. Another risk was being fired on from low flying Allied planes, which happened many times. We did not understand why that happened, since from the air, civilians with bikes could easily be distinguished from German soldiers.

An uncle who lived in the city of Utrecht was a police officer. One night, following a special assignment as he called it, he returned to his station with his uniform dotted with white flour. 'All right,' his fellow-policemen told him, 'if you manage to get some small bags of flour for us as well, we will not turn you in'. It is one of thousands of anecdotes which reflect people's extreme efforts to get hold of badly-needed food and fuel, and what unexpected results such efforts might have. Many others cut down trees, which in the Netherlands is illegal without special permission. In Amsterdam and The Hague, boys took paving slab size pieces of wood from between tram tracks, and put them on the fire at home. These were tarred however. Burning them in the living or kitchen often resulted in a bad smell and lots of smoke, forcing people to open up their windows.

One day in January 1945, my mother returned from the baker, though I don't remember if she was with or without bread. What I do remember is what she reported: 'The baker has said that he could only bake bread with the flour he has had to sweep from the floor. And then he said, "Enjoy your meal."'

Chapter Nineteen

Freed – 5 May, 1945

The Germans sank into defeat, precisely as my grandmother had told them, one day in December 1944. 'You Germans will lose this war,' she told one officer. 'Why?', he asked. 'Because you persecute the Jews. They are God's people!' The German laughed in her face. 'Do you know what we will do?' he asked her. 'We will celebrate Christmas through the chimney!' He was referring to the ovens of Auschwitz. It was a shocking answer and she repeated this story a few times in later years.

The Canadian 1st Army and parts of the British 2nd Army entered the Netherlands through Emmerich and continued through a narrow, secret route near Dinxperlo on 27 March 1945, southeast of Arnhem. This was the last day that the Germans fired V-2s at Britain from The Hague, one of the two mobile launching places in this country. One of the monsters killed a British civilian (in Orpington, Kent), the very last victim. The second V-2 caused no injury on impact. Three days earlier, Montgomery's 21st Army Group had crossed the Rhine near Wesel – operations Plunder and Varsity.

Surprisingly, the Allied liberation of the Netherlands in 1945 took almost six weeks, despite the German forces being tired of the war, depleted in numbers, and only occupying the north half of the country. British and Canadian forces, however, advanced very carefully. They wanted to save as many soldiers' lives as possible at this final stage of the war.

Doetinchem was the first Dutch city taken by the Allies in this final offensive on 1 April. It was a few kilometres from Germany. From there, forces were deployed in several directions. While the axis of the British 2nd Army was aimed at Oldenburg, Germany, its left flank advanced to the north of the Netherlands. The 1st Canadian Army, including the British 49th (West Riding) Infantry Division, took the Netherlands. They advanced to Arnhem first and enjoyed a sweet revenge when the city, albeit severely battered, was captured in the ensuing fights, from 13 to 15 April. This time they entered Arnhem from two sides. One was west of the city, in the area where surviving British troops had crossed the Rhine to escape in 1944. The other was east of the city. The Germans, meanwhile, had reinforced the fortress at the IJssel bridge near Arnhem where my father had been stationed in 1940. Ironically, while the Dutch defence was aimed at Germany in 1940, the German defence of 1945 aimed in exactly the same direction because it was from here, this time, that the Canadians came from.

Crowds cheer a Humber reconnaissance vehicle of the British 49th (West Riding) Division, entering and liberating Utrecht city, 7 May 1945. The site is *Potterstraat*. (*Photographer: Alex Stirton; Library and Archives Canada a133323*)

This second Battle of Arnhem took three days. The Germans deployed heavy fire from the high ground north of the city. The fighting caused considerable damage to the city again – the third time since September 1944. The Canadian 1st Army was instrumental in the liberation of the Netherlands. It participated in the ultimate liberation of Arnhem, Utrecht, Hilversum and several other Dutch towns in the west.

On the next day, the Germans blew up the dikes of Wieringermeer Polder in North-Holland province, between Enkhuizen and Den Helder. The whole area was flooded. All food factories, houses and buildings were destroyed. It took until December 1945 until the area was dry for a second time, while the two places where the Germans struck are still visible. A remarkable record is that while in Germany a few cities were destroyed almost totally, Wieringermeer suffered more than any of them. As the map shows, the Germans inundated very many more areas in the Netherlands.

Sometime in the second half of April, we at Breukelen suddenly heard heavy field guns in a far distance. They were Canadian guns. The end was really near now, but hunger and terror in the west continued and caused more victims every day. Sunday, 29 April 1945, however, was different. Hitler married Eva Braun on this day and committed suicide on the next. More important for us was that RAF and – a few days later the USAAF – bombers started the first of over 5,300 sorties to the Netherlands to drop food. A few days later, Canadian Army trucks entered the still occupied Netherlands to bring food and a lot more badly-needed supplies by the Dutch.

The Dutch government in exile, fully aware of this misery, had started to stockpile food supplies back in 1943. A big problem, of course, was how to get these to the Dutch. Secret negotiations between high level Allied and German military, early in 1945, were inevitable but very odd. Both parties hated and mistrusted each other. The Germans believed that they could hold out for the next year at least and nothing prevented them from starving more Dutch citizens. They suggested that the British were planning a sneaky Allied invasion of the Netherlands, rather than just to drop food. They also suggested that the bombers would include spy planes, weapon drops or even an airborne landing again. In turn and more realistically, the Allies wanted to prevent all those tons and tons of food to be dropped in crates or sacks, with no parachutes, from being stolen and taken to Germany, and also

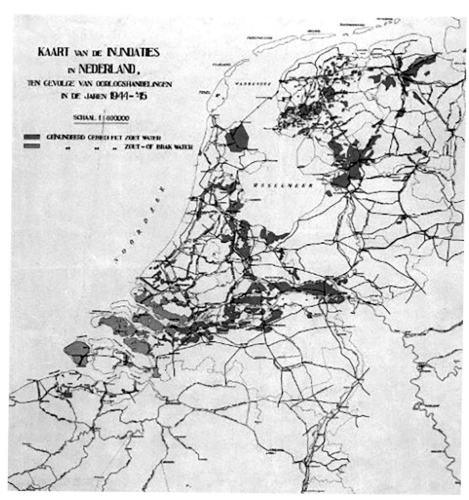

Map of forced flooding in the Netherlands, 1944–1945. It shows that 9 percent of the land was flooded in 10 out of 11 provinces. (Today's 12th province, Flevoland, was reclaimed in the IJssel Lake.) Wieringermeer Polder in the northwest and the large area between Arnhem and Nijmegen, Betuwe, are two of the largest areas that were deliberately flooded by the occupier.

making sure that no Germans fired at the low flying aircraft. In the end, the Germans also required that Allied crews took no cameras with them.

A few airmen ignored this. Most were happy to have a different assignment as they dropped 11,000 tons of small food packs. Manna was the name of the RAF operation, Chowhound the one used by the USAAF. Officially eleven fields were selected for these drops in the 'Hunger Winter area', as finally agreed by Hitler's governor, Seyss-Inquart. In reality, however, there would have been more drops, as I remember vividly the drop at Breukelen. Half the village stood near the (unofficial) dropping zone, screaming and dancing for joy when one or a few slow and very low flying bombers dropped the packs. In all, over thirty British Lancaster squadrons and eleven USAAF Bomb Groups (400 bombers) were involved in the entire operation, but also two Australian and one Polish squadron. There were no better names than Manna and Chowhound for an operation of this kind.

German surrender in the Netherlands was announced on Friday, 4 May 1945, effective the next day at 6am. My parents permitted me to leave the

An Allied bomber dropping food.

house into the back yard, at six that particular morning, as I wanted to see myself how it looked to be free. Nothing exceptional drew my attention. I also opened the door of the shed. Inside it was dark as usual. Was that all, what they called 'to be free'?

Things became a lot clearer in the next few days. People danced and cheered in the streets of Breukelen, even before a single Allied soldier was spotted, but more so when on the morning of 9 May, a number of Allied scout cars and trucks rolled onto the town's *Markt*. Within minutes, seemingly, they were surrounded and welcomed by most of the local population, as pictures show. A few hours later people lined Main Street to watch and scoff at a number of females, sitting on handcarts, their heads shaven bald, tar and white feathers on their skin, surrounded by men pushing the handcarts. They had fraternized with Germans in whatever way and they had to be derided, like they were anywhere else in continental West Europe in those days. My father thought it *prachtig* (beautiful) as he said a few times. To me it was rather disgusting. What had this to do with 'being free', if anything?

One afternoon, I joined two or three Canadian soldiers who taught me my first English words; Hello, good morning, good evening. Quite a different kind of experience was when a captured German, one prisoner within a small group, offered me a piece of bread. My father saw the encounter from inside our house as I was at the end of the back yard, and he took pride (as he told me much later) in seeing my refusal.

Maybe on the same day, a few Germans strolling in the street, prior to being taken into POW camps, rang at my grandmother's front door without a trifle of embarrassment for their conduct in the past five years. '*Bitte haben Sie Kartoffeln für uns?*' they begged. 'Do you have potatoes for us, please?' The answer was *No* and it was not a lie, but had we had any, we would scarcely have given them anything.

Red, white and blue flags, the national colours, as well as orange banners (Orange-Nassau) were waving from houses. My mother bought orange paper and made a very nice looking Scottish-type beret for me. Jealous peasant boys took it and tore it apart on the same day. And then, one day, there was an endless looking column of German POWs marching towards Utrecht city, 12km (7 miles) to the south. A couple of weeks earlier, some Germans had tied four or five Resistance workers to the rear of a truck on the same road, but outside Breukelen. Then they had started driving at high speed, dragging their victims apart until they died. I didn't see this myself, but my father told me about this atrocity. But now it was different.

German POWs marched through Breukelen and were called Nazi-dogs, thieves, traitors and all other sorts of names by the locals. At the same time, a few Allied tanks entered Breukelen from Utrecht. They were enormous in my small mind, they were taller than most Germans tanks I had seen before. But then, the Germans were ordered to stop and make a quarter turn left, in order to pay tribute to the Allies. Which they did; they were Germans after all and *Befehl ist Befehl,* an order is an order, just do it! This caused another cheerful outbreak of joy among those who watched the scene.

Millions in Europe were far from their homes at the end of the war; Allied POW; German POW in Allied camps; non-German prisoners; Jews; Slavs and other ethnic minorities, all those who had narrowly escaped from being killed in Nazi-camps, forced labourers and – of course – the millions of Allied soldiers who had defeated Nazi-Germany. Around 12 million Germans were evicted from Slav countries in the next few years – none of them was home. The same was true for this relatively small group of citizens from Arnhem and beyond. But we were not allowed to return. The city which had been a front-line city two, if not three times, including the winter, had to be cleared of explosives, countless booby traps and other dangerous materials first. Reportedly, there were about 900,000 devices at least found in the Arnhem area alone. They also included items that had been destroyed such as aircraft, gliders, tanks, jeeps, field guns and all other kinds of heavy armament. Not the kind of city decoration most towns appreciate when a war is over.

My parents, like others in our district, were allowed to re-enter Arnhem by early August. As NS were heavily damaged in virtually every way, there were still no train services and only 30,000 private cars were left in the country. So, we were allowed on a barge to return to Arnhem. A nice and unique trip which took most of a day in the bright summer of 1945. But then what a mess and destruction we faced when we stepped onto a quay of the Rhine in our city, at a point where we could proceed no longer, as the Rhine bridge barred the way. And what an enormous collection of ruins, charred walls, junk, trash, rubble, broken windows, bad smelling houses, and shambles it all was, in every street we passed.

The Wilshire Regiment monument, Arnhem.

By evening we arrived at our own house. The sight and the interior were stunning. All windows were broken, doors swung on their hinges, or had disappeared. Furniture was gone or broken. A grenade, presumably of Canadian origin, had hit our kitchen and had exploded on the stairs. It had caused strange damage. The shelter in our back yard was gone. There was a bad, penetrating smell of burnt metal all over the house, in spite of all the fresh air that could enter from the west and leave it at the east side during the past months. We found that those who had been in our house had not flushed the toilet, as they had no water. There were also traces and smells of vermin, alive and dead. A wooden floor was broken. People clearly had been looking for objects of value.

Most furniture was destroyed or non-existent, including table-chairs and our beds. My own wooden bed had been sawn into two halves. One half to be found in the back yard, the other half was gone. There was not even a mattress. My parents managed to make something up into a bed for me. But lacking any blankets and by way of a joke, mum tucked me in with a newspaper for a blanket. Some liberation!

Epilogue

'Arnhem' was a failure and those who survived free were withdrawn. But 'Arnhem' was not a victory for the Germans, despite them proudly announcing it as such. Nor was it a 'defeat of the British Army', as the Germans emphasized determinedly in their news reports. Sure, there was a German repulse of the British and Polish in the Arnhem area with great psychological impact on all those involved and living there. But, as the German propaganda stated boldly: *'Das Blatt wendet sich!'*, The leaf is turning; typical dictator speak. Since D-Day, the Germans had been defeated on all major fronts in Europe. They could no longer prevail in head-on clashes of about equally sized and armed forces, even though the failure to establish a bridge-head in Arnhem had serious consequences, not just for the Dutch population in the area until the end of the war.

For many years, the British involved in the Arnhem battles have felt defeated. It is true that they were not victorious and they did not succeed in establishing the essential bridge-head. Their commitment of a division and a Polish brigade was too small, however, to have a chance. Germans were already in the area and were made available by train in huge numbers. The British were deprived of 85 per cent of their supplies from the beginning, there were no reinforcements and they were not relieved in time. Three-quarters of the British and Polish force were swept away in less than a week. This was largely due to inadequate leadership from behind the frontline. Arnhem was a bridge too far for generals like Montgomery and Browning, and the Germans reaped the benefit.

Meanwhile these Allies were part of a large force, the 2nd Army, which was not counterattacked, defeated, or forced to retreat. Not even half way, back to their starting point in Belgium, which was what Model aimed for. The Germans did not retake a bridge at Nijmegen. It is fair to say that in the Arnhem area, the Germans only repulsed the airborne vanguard of the advance – XXX Corps – of the larger British 2nd Army. Arnhem fell short as a starting point from which to attack north Germany and the industrial Ruhr Area in the next months, which was the first reason for the attack all the way to Arnhem. Unfortunately, it is also true that a week after Market Garden had begun, there was no starting point to end the war by Christmas 1944, as Montgomery had believed possible.

A bridge-head north of the Rhine would also have been a starting point to eliminate the V-2 rocket and V-1 buzz bomb launching site in The Hague (and Hook of Holland later), as Montgomery had been ordered to attempt by his government. Having lost this bridge-head, these sites provoked the Germans to continue direct attacks on Britain, Belgium and France which cost the lives of many thousands in those countries. People were lost who for decades might have had a wide array of useful contributions to the post-war world, as numerous records show of those who have survived. Also, the occupying German forces in the west and north of the Netherlands were not contained or eliminated. This enabled the Germans to continue terrorising the Dutch and bring much destruction to the country, even after the German surrender. The continued occupation also caused large scale starvation in the west of the country.

The heavy fighting that had started on the afternoon of Sunday, 17 September became more intense over the next few days. The three positions held by the Airborne divisions each quickly became untenable because of the overwhelming and increasing power the Germans deployed, and the lack of relief from XXX Corps. As early as Tuesday the 19th my father was one among many who expressed some doubts about the outcome. More and more heavy German reinforcements and troops rolled into Arnhem. Reinforcements in men and supplies by air fell short as well, or fell into German hands.

'*Ik ben bang dat het niet gaat lukken*', my dad said a couple of times: I'm afraid it won't work. He certainly was not the only one in our street, our city, with fear growing. People referred to 'Dempsey's tanks' then. The unseen tanks were believed to be 'stuck in the soft clay of the Betuwe' as people guessed. But the road from Nijmegen to Elst and on to Arnhem was a good one in those days, made of concrete slabs, unchanged until long after the war. An abandoned stretch just south of Elst is still in place.

An abandoned road near Elst, similar to how it would have looked in 1944.

A broker of food supplies, temporarily staying in the Arnhem area, Dr W. Majoewsky who originated from Amsterdam, was another of those observing and keeping a diary. He was 'stuck' in Armhem, meaning that due to the railway strike, he could not return home by train. He observed the first British POWs, as he understood them to be from their unfamiliar dresses. His diary is kept in the Provincial Archives in Arnhem. On Tuesday, 19 September he wrote:

'As to the military performances, it was known publicly that there was little movement in the battle. The combats went up and down in the city. The bridge, in English hands soon after their arrival, is said to be in German hands again. Monday, until about 13.00pm, a heavy fog still was over the city which again resulted in inability to drop Allied supplies, while heavy German equipment kept rolling towards Arnhem.'

No, the bridge was not in German hands again on Monday. Frost's battalion at the north ramp was fighting like hell to keep it, while the Germans did the same to retake it from the city side alone. Bittrich believed that British soldiers were not very good at attacking as he told his men, but very good at defending themselves. He was thinking about the British involvement at Kasserine Pass when he said the latter, while conveniently overlooking the final days of Alamein for the former. In Arnhem, Frost and his men amazed the Germans, as some have declared later, for their perseverance, literally until they ran out of bullets.

Dr Majoewsky says:

'About 14.00pm we observed the first POWs, about a 100 men. Dressed in some sort of overall, dotted brown and red, while they also wore red-brown berets on one ear [berets were not worn by German soldiers or the Dutch, prewar] … remarkable differences in soldier's lengths. Heavy and slightly built men could be seen. At about 15.00pm the heavy fog was rising. Flying resumed until 18.00pm. Also, parachutists were dropped [west of Wolfheze]. No German aircraft in sight then. Meanwhile we had observed a few English cars [jeeps] captured by Germans. They attracted us because of their high whining, speeds and smooth running of engines.'

Meanwhile, the thunderous noise of heavy explosions, firing and fighting in several parts of Arnhem and from the Betuwe across the Rhine could be heard all over town which included our own street in an eastern district. On the 20th, he noted:

'On Wednesday morning, again no change of conditions while we were taken by unpleasant surprise, to see about 150 POWs. We not only got a feeling that there was little progress, but even more that things were going wrong. Heavy German artillery was positioned [on the high ground] around Arnhem and the screaming of grenades flying across the city, aimed at the Betuwe and Nijmegen, was to be heard uninterruptedly. In most streets joining Velperweg all kinds of armour were in place, heavily camouflaged under the trees. If the 2nd Army does not show up very soon, the paratroopers and airborne forces can not hold out, how bravely they resist.'

But this is what they did, in part, as Bittrich had explained to his men at the beginning of the Battle.

On Thursday morning – a little over three days and nights after the north ramp of the Rhine bridge was captured – Frost and what was left of his battalion, about 400 men, had to give up. Over 200 men at least had been killed or wounded. This included Frost who was seriously injured. Their ammunitions were depleted, there were no more supplies, there was no contact with other battalions or the tactical HQ at Oosterbeek. The exchanges of fire at the bridge ceased. The men near the bridge, dead tired, exhausted, wounded, hungry and thirsty, felt worse than miserable. Those alive were taken prisoner. It was the disappointing end of a gallant battle that had taken too long.

Arnhem and Oosterbeek became front-line cities during the following winter, but the outcome and the damage were never held against the British and the Poles by civilians in the area. This includes, for instance, my grandfather's premises which were reduced to rubble leaving him no business and nowhere to live. One former British combatant expressed his astonishment about this attitude on Dutch television one day: 'Their cities in shambles and they call us liberators!' he said. Yes, we do and we still do. This attitude even prevails amongst many born after the war. Obviously, the damage initially resulted from the Allied airborne landings and the ensuing fighting. But war exacts a high price in lives and property lost. No peace without effort – and more effort was needed to prevent war and restore peace. Secondly, much damage resulted from random and uncalled for German actions. Thirdly, more damage was done when the city was relieved in April 1945.

'They came to defeat evil and win peace,' as a British Army officer correctly stated on 19 September 2015. This officer, whose name and rank was not recorded, addressed an audience at the annual commemoration of the 1944 air landings at Ginkel Heath between Arnhem and Ede. One British soldier remembered that, after landing, the advance to Arnhem was so 'quiet and calm' that it seemed like 'an exercise in England' as he said. But this wasn't for long. The number of men and their arms in 1944 were too limited to hold out against all the Germans were able to deploy, even though there were supposed to be enough to take the entire city of Arnhem, including the bridge until relieved. Arnhem appeared a bridge too far for Browning's strategy and for Horrocks' tanks; while at the bridge it was a battle too hard for Frost and his men against the Germans.

Something exceptional had happened at St. Elisabeth's hospital, meanwhile. However badly the Germans behaved towards everyone, there were some among them who behaved more than decently towards all wounded soldiers, including British and Polish. The hospital was taken by the British on Sunday, 17 September. Wounded soldiers were taken in and cared for by British doctors and their staff, while the Dutch medical staff took care of Dutch victims. The Germans took the hospital again on Monday. Their surgeons arrived with them and the British medics left, leaving their wounded. But then, the hospital was retaken by the British for a while and their surgeons came back again. Finally, the Germans, their medics and attendants took over for a second time during these hostilities. Rather than leaving, the British now stayed and worked next to the Germans. Local citizens believed this was a miracle, rather than a 'natural thing'. It transpired later that this situation instigated from orders issued by Bittrich himself, which was even more miraculous.

This was also confirmed long after the war by Albert Speer, Hitler's Minister of Armaments and War Production. Speer paid a visit to Bittrich in Arnhem after the conclusion of Market Garden. He arrived at Bittrich's base to find the General in a state of fury. Speer later wrote in his diary that it was Bittrich who had permitted the British to continue their medical care behind the German lines during the battle. Bittrich had also permitted at least one Allied field hospital behind the German lines in the later stage of the siege of the Perimeter at Oosterbeek. He had allowed a few pauses in the fighting to recover wounded from both sides. The reason for Bittrich's anger, according to Speer, was that other SS members had taken the opportunity to kill captured British soldiers and American pilots in a field hospital. Bittrich was furious again after the war when he was charged with these killings, but when he had explained and proved his actions, these charges were dropped.

All over the area there was extremely heavy shooting all around, including German field guns and tanks. There were German fighter planes overhead and there was, of course, the shouting as much as the screaming of fighting, wounded and dying soldiers of both sides. In our eastern part of Arnhem the heavy explosions of the battle could easily be heard. It stands to reason that I was no longer allowed to go into the street, not even into the back yard of our house.

Allied, German and civilian losses during and following the Battle of Arnhem may have amounted to more than 15,000, including 6,854 POWs, based on figures available today at the Hartenstein Airborne Museum of Oosterbeek. They included over 8,600 Allies on the ground and as air force personnel. Not included are 60 who did not survive the German POW camps. Next, about 450 to 500 civilians lost their lives, but several more may not have survived the forcible eviction of Arnhem and other towns in the area during the next eight months. In total, 1,511 Allied soldiers of 1944 and April 1945 are buried at the Oosterbeek War Cemetery. Of these, 1,392 are British, 73 Polish, 32 Canadians, 6 Dutch, 4 Australian, 4 New Zealanders and 253 are unknown Allied soldiers. Another 36 British are buried at Moscowa, Arnhem's municipal cemetery. At least one British soldier of Market Garden is known to be buried elsewhere.

This exception is a British sergeant, James Gibbons. A caretaker at nearby Bennekom found his body among others in 1944. He found a note in the man's uniform on which Gibbons had written that he preferred to be buried in a Catholic graveyard. Obviously, this last wish was carried out accordingly. Gibbons' grave was adopted by a Mrs. W.H.M. Peelen of Bennekom, many years later. Her adoption is in line with those of most graveyards at Oosterbeek by many hundreds of young school children from Oosterbeek and beyond, as many years as they prefer. Young school children succeed older adopters, even today.

There have been adoptions ever since a ceremony held on 17 September 1945, after most remains, until then buried at different private or public places in the area, had been exhumed or recovered and united at Oosterbeek since 1945. A few British who survived the battle were buried at Oosterbeek after dying decades later in Britain, as they wanted to be returned among their comrades of 1944.

There must be a few words about the Poles killed in the Arnhem area, buried at Oosterbeek. Their remains were prepared to be returned to Poland in 1946–7. However, the shipment of coffins was refused by Polish authorities at the country's border for reasons that these soldiers had been

British paratroopers surrender in Arnhem. Humiliated at the time, but respected to this day. A closer look reveals the anger in the eyes and faces of the 1st and 2nd Airborne. (*Bundesarchiv Bild 146-2005-0077 by Erich Wenzel, Sep. 1944*)

fighting together with the British. It was a clear and really unexpected token of disregard for humans by the communists, the new 'people's regime' of Poland. The coffins were returned to Oosterbeek and only then buried alongside the British soldiers.

The Dutch didn't want the German dead of 1944–45 to be put to rest in the Arnhem area. They were exhumed after the war to be taken away. They were buried at the IJsselstein cemetery in the province of Brabant, which was reserved for any German who died in the Netherlands, if not repatriated by their descendants. The number of German losses in the Netherlands is not known.

In 1969, British veterans suggested ending the annual commemoration ceremony at Oosterbeek. It was denied emphatically. Several ceremonies are still held in the Arnhem area in late September every year, when many British visit the area. In most cases – depending on the weather – the commemoration includes a parachute landing at historic Ginkel Heath, near Ede. For many years some of these paratroopers were original British veterans.

Securing a bridge-head in Arnhem very much looks like a military rush job instead of being aware that Arnhem was most serious part of Market Garden. As a result, Arnhem became subordinate to the entire operation instead of its key. A bridge too far for the capacities of those who had made the plan and who had spoken the prophetic words in case of a failure. A bridge too far and a result too small at the expense of many thousands of military Allied lives.

Sources

Airborne Museum 'Hartenstein', Oosterbeek.
Gelders Archief, Arnhem.
Koninklijke Bibliotheek (Royal Netherlands Library), The Hague.
Museum 1940–1945, Dordrecht.
Netherlands Intitute for Military History, The Hague.
NIOD (Netherlands Institute for war, holocaust and genocide studies), Amsterdam.

.

Bibliography

Chronik 1944: Tag fuer Tag in Wort und Bild, (Bertelsmann Lexicon Verlag, Guetersloh, Germany, 1988).

Economische en sociale kroniek der oorlogsjaren 1940–1945, (W. de Haan, Utrecht, 1947).

Altes, A. Korthals, *Luchtgevaar*, (Sijthoff, Amsterdam, 1984).

Boscawen, Robert, *Armoured Guardsmen: A War Diary, June 1944–April 1945* (Pen & Sword, Barnsley, 2001 (2010).

Brinkhuis, Alfons E., *Fatale aanval, 22 februari 1944*, (Antiquariaat Van Hoorn, Nijmegen, 1984).

Butler, Rupert, *Illustrierte Geschichte der Gestapo*, (Brechtermünz Verlag, Augsburg, 1997).

Clark, Lloyd, *Arnhem: Operation Market Garden, September 1944*, (History Press, UK, 2002).

Eisenhower, General Dwight D., *Kruistocht door Europa*, (Servire Den Haag, 1949).

Farrar-Hockley, Anthony, *Airborne Carpet: Operation Market Garden* (Macdonald & Co., London, 1969).

Fischer, Fritz, *Griff nach der Weltmach*, (Droste Verlag, Duesseldorf,1961).

Frequin, Louis, Henri Knap, W.H. Kruiderink, *Arnhems Kruisweg* (Promotor, Amsterdam, 1946).

Hibbert, Christoffer, *The Battle of Arnhem*, (Sijthoff, Leiden, 1963).

Hillgruber, Andreas, *Hitlers Strategie*, (Bernard & Graefe Verlag, Bonn, 1993).

Hitler, Adolf, *Mein Kampf* (Copy in Royal Netherlands Library, The Hague).

Huurman, C., *Spoorwegbedrijf in oorlogstijd, 1939–45*, (Uquilair Den Bosch, 2001).

Maan, Ingrid, *Weggemoffeld!*, (Fagus, IJzerlo NL, 2015).

van Iddeking, P.R.A., *Arnhem 44/45* (Gelderse boekhandel, Arnhem, 1981).

Visser, Lt. Col. J., *Vijf dagen oorlog in Nederland, 10–14 mei 1940*, (Van Cleef, The Hague, 1946).

Wagenaar, Aad, *Rotterdam Mei 1940*, (Meppel, Netherlands, 1970).

Zentner, Dr Christian, *Der Zweite Weltkrieg: Daten, Fakten, Kommentare*, (Moewig, Auflage, 1998).